When Fairy Tales Kill

When Fairy Tales Kill

✦

The Origins and Transmission of Antisemitic Beliefs

Steven K. Baum

iUniverse, Inc.
New York Bloomington Shanghai

When Fairy Tales Kill
The Origins and Transmission of Antisemitic Beliefs

iUniverse books may be ordered through booksellers or by contacting:

iUniverse
1663 Liberty Drive
Bloomington, IN 47403
www.iuniverse.com
1-800-Authors (1-800-288-4677)

Because of the dynamic nature of the Internet, any Web addresses or links contained in this book may have changed since publication and may no longer be valid.

ISBN: 978-0-595-48140-8 (pbk)
ISBN: 978-0-595-60235-3 (ebk)

Printed in the United States of America

For
Henry and Rita Muroff
Jack Baum and Alice Nemeth

When we first heard of the political myths, we found them so absurd and incongruous, so fantastic and ludicrous, that we could hardly be prevailed upon to take them seriously. By the end of the war, however, it had become clear to all of us that this was a great mistake ... The mythical monsters were not entirely destroyed. They were used for the creation of a new universe and they still survive in this universe.

Ernst Cassirer, philosopher (1874–1945)

Contents

Acknowledgments

The author wishes to thank the following persons for their assistance with the bibliography: Sara Grosveld at the Vidal Sassoon International Center for the Study of Antisemitism Hebrew University, Jerusalem; Adaire Klein, Director of Library and Archival Services, (Los Angeles) and Shimon Samuels, Director of International Relations, Simon Wiesenthal Center (Paris); Moira Lorraine Smith, Folklore Librarian and Hasan El Shamy, Department of Folklore and Ethnomusicology at Indiana University; Leo Greenbaum and Yeshaya Metal at YIVO; Mark and Randi Biederman, Audrey Hummelen, R.J. Barb Silver, Julianna Lerner, Elizabeth Isack, Jordan, Josh and Shaina, Gail Stangor, Charles Clarke, Linda Koltonow, Marcia Littell, Neal Rosenberg, Maggi Eastwood, the work of the late Stephen Feinstein and Ginette Baum who inspired me to use fiction to advance the understanding of antisemitism and to whom this book is truly dedicated.

Introduction

For centuries, children have been delighted to hear bedtime tales of wonder and magic as parents tucked them in at night. They have heard the legends and dreamt of enchanted woods, flying unicorns, and beanstalks that would rise to the sky. They have learned of princesses rescued by brave knights and have drifted off to sleep comforted and contained by their parent's presence.

Pure as snow, "the lasting security of folk legends represent the most reassuring and most refreshing of God's gifts to man," said the Brothers Grimm. The tales themselves were sensational—the stuff of whimsy and fantasy. Tellers of those tales were loving parents, nannies, and grandparents, who likely were not aware of the Jewish themes in the background. Few saw politics in the folklore, and most were unconcerned. Some believed the tales to be true, while others did not think that it would matter. After all, every story has its villains.

But in the history of antisemitism, it does matter. How are we to account for hundreds of thousands of Jews killed before 1939 because of floating cultural and religious myths? How are we to explain why the Nazis revised key fairy tales to be used in their "educational" campaigns directed at children? Why do government-controlled newspapers continue to promote antisemitc myths throughout Iran and the Arab Middle East? [1]

Grotesque as goblins and slicker than Satan, Jews portrayed in storybooks personified evil, but with one exception: Jews also existed in the real world. To be sure, other storyline characters were portrayed as evil and existed in real life—inn-keepers, for example. But the church and state additionally told only tales of the nefarious ways of the Jews. The combination was lethal. Most Christians and Muslims knew of the Jews only by their storyline reputation, which was so real to them that Jews were to be shunned, contained, or even slain.

Cultural anthropologists will remind you that Jews had a minor role in folktales, that their depiction was ambivalent, and that such tales traveled in taverns, family gatherings, and social settings. But eventually, those tales reached children and grew to be reflected in marchen, children's games, oral narrative, myths, and legends. It could also be included in our definition caricatures, slogans, and limericks, as well as in sermons, art, theater, movies, graffiti, jokes, innocuous slips of the tongue, and in musical, customary, and material traditional expressions. In this sense, the world of myths and the stereotypes they engender is ubiquitous.[2]

"Legend telling is often a fundamentally political act," observed folklorist Bill Ellis.[3] And politics were not a stranger to constructing the fable image of the Jews. As this compilation will reveal, that image is overwhelmingly negative. The image reflects the ongoing social narrative of Jews passed down from generation to generation. The antisemitc narrative seems to travel along the grapevine like paranormal and supernatural phenomena. One historian likened antisemitism to ghosts (Pinsker 1882). The Third Reich's antisemitc propaganda merely embellished what had saturated Europe's cultural air for centuries. After exhaustive examination of Nazi propaganda, historian Norman Cohn concluded that "the drive to exterminate Jews sprang from a quasi-demonological superstition." (1996, p. xii)

Superstition and antisemitism have always been bedfellows. Non-Jewish minds linked Jews with bad forces. After a while, this association became more automatic, connecting an unpleasant feeling to the word "Jew." Statistical and scientific tests such as the Implicit Association Test proved the link, as did correlation studies (Baum and Rudski 2008). The stage was set for an ongoing storyline of a dangerous people, a national narrative that pervades culture—even those cultures where no Jews reside.

Throughout this work, the focus will remain on the culturally imagined aspect of Jews—what others have at times called mythical. For instance, Jews in real life may or may not act as the mythical Jew. Yet it is common knowledge that Jews are said to be taking over the planet—an unlikely circumstance given that Jews constitute one-twenty-fourth of 1 percent of the world's population. Although the imaginary Jews are alleged to be of inferior stock, real Jews are among those with the highest literacy rates, accounting in recent years for one-fifth of the Nobel Prizes in medicine and related sciences. The fantasy Jews are said to be engaged in sinister and nefarious acts, yet the real Jews' crime rates are consistently lower than those of other social groups. The reality of Jews has little to do with the fantasy. However, people often prefer fantasy.

This book will examine how folk beliefs derived from antisemitc myths remain in the back of one's social mind, waiting to be exploited for political purposes. The triggering mechanism could be a demagogue, or a religious cleric, or a next-door neighbor. But there seems to be a saturation point where "everybody knows" who is to blame, after which clarion calls for genocide begin.

For years, politics was indicted. There were clearly good reasons to examine fascistic governments, authoritarian thinking, and despotism. Religion was not held to the same standard, however, since it was considered private and personal. In democracies, religion was protected, as was the speech that went along with one's religious beliefs.

After 9/11, we now understand that religion provides some of the best sources of hate. One can examine any of the one hundred ninety eight passages from the New Testament or the fifty five antisemitc suras of the Koran and Hadith and recognize that disdain for Jews has been sanctioned from above (e.g., Simon of Trent, the Patron Saint of antisemitism).

But the antisemitc belief may have been something learned in grade school, by way of something as innocuous as a Mother Goose poem (pre-1939 versions, emphasis added).

> Old Mother Goose,
> When she wanted to wander,
> Would ride through the air,
> On a very fine gander.
> Mother Goose had a house,
> 'Twas built in a wood,
> Where an owl at the door,
> As sentinel stood.
> She had a son Jack,
> A plain-looking lad,
> He was not very good,
> Nor yet very bad.
> She sent him to market,
> A live goose he bought;
> "Here, mother," says he, "It will not go for naught."
> Jack's goose and her gander
> Soon grew very fond,
> They'd both eat together
> And swim in one pond.
> Jack found one morning,
> As I have been told,
> His goose had laid him
> An egg of pure gold.
> Jack ran to his mother,
> The news for to tell;
> She called him a good boy,
> And said it was well.

Jack sold his gold egg
To a rogue of a Jew,
Who cheated him out of
The half of his due.
Then Jack went a-courting
A lady so gay,
As fair as the lily,
And sweet as the may.
The Jew and the Squire
Then came at his back,
And began to belabor
The sides of poor Jack.
They threw the gold egg
In the midst of the sea;
But Jack he jumped in,
And got it back presently.
The Jew got the goose,
Which he vowed he would kill,
Resolving at once
His pockets to fill.
Jack's mother came in,
And caught the goose soon,
And, mounting its back,
Flew up to the moon.[3]

Regarding antisemitc themes, the Grimm Brothers are not above reproach. One reviewer recalls reading their version of *Cinderella*.

> In that telling, the wicked stepmother, unable to force her daughters' big feet into the glass slipper, slices off the toes of one and squeezes the foot of the other "until the blood came." Eventually, the stepmother herself is forced into shoes of red-hot iron and dances until she drops down dead. "None of this shocked me as a child. More disturbingly, I was also unfazed by the book's relentless antisemitism. I wasn't terribly sure what a Jew was ... but [their] stories made it pretty clear they weren't to be trusted.[4]

The compilation of folktales assembled here is not comprehensive and may not reflect the salience or prevalence of antisemitism within a particular culture. For instance, Iceland has no antisemitc folklore, per se. At the same time, as much as 75 percent of that nation believes in trolls, grogs, goblins, and fairies. But their infamous trolls have several traits, which parallel the Jew. One wonders how the trolls' traits came to be. Did tales of the Jew morph into trolls?

The purpose of this book will be to examine in greater detail how folklore fuels and foments antisemitc beliefs, and how people confuse fact and fiction. It is a tale of the Jew who does not exist in real life—the Jew who is not really there. It tells how real Jews are killed to eradicate the imaginary ones. This is a story of the origins and transmission of antisemitc beliefs, and how folktales and legends kill.

1

What's an Imaginary Jew?

Volkish ideas are still with us beneath the surface, ready to be used in those extreme crises which mankind constantly manufactures.
    —George Mosse

"Once upon a time ... " the classic fairy tale opening seems benign enough. But what generally follows is a tale of enchantment complemented with morals and lessons. Myths offer simple solutions to life's problems, encouraging us to divide the world into good people and bad people, and to label actions and beliefs as right or wrong. Creation, the end of the world, afterlife, floods, supernatural beings, morality, love, death, and the fall from grace are not only the stuff of great novels—they are folkloric themes that appear in all cultures.

Folklore is defined as information communicated from person to person and from generation to generation by word of mouth (Ashliman 2004). The experts are less certain as to their transmission or when the earliest fairy tales, myths, and legends came into being—their origins predate recorded history. Some scholars believe the first myths originated in ancient India. Mutating over time through multiple retellings, these tales were revived through the centuries, passed along by travelers, sailors, pilgrims, merchants, soldiers, and others. By the eighteenth century, popular tales and stories found a new audience among the poor and uneducated that bought the wares of traveling dealers, called chapmen. Chapmen distributed popular tales and stories bound in chap, or cheap little booklets.

Though many ancient fairy tales grew out of rituals celebrating the cycles of nature and the seasons, others served as a means to reinforce societal values. Legends, myths, folklore, and fairy tales are not as politically neutral as one might hope. Interest in the politics of *Little Black Sambo* and Grimm Brothers' fairy tales are just beginning to be examined by scholars (Kamenetsky 1972; Lipson 2001).

For instance, the Nazis liked folklore and spent hours advancing their political agenda to fit with fairy tales and fables (Dow and Lixfeld 1994; Kamenetsky 1972, 1979; Mieder 1997). Judith Proud (1997) has examined the fairy tale revision from neutral to antisemitc in Vichy, France. Her colleague, Wolfgang Mieder (1982), further demonstrated the great lengths Nazis went to in order to write out Jews as part of the folk/volk, and write them in as aliens, to manufacture folklore as simple proverbs. They used verbal folklore—especially fairy tales, legends, jokes, and proverbs, as quoted—to prove that the healthy folk mind had long recognized the Jew's negative qualities.

Legends and Social Beliefs

While real Jews may bear no resemblance to the Jews of collective imaginations, the *social* narrative does not make such distinction. In the *social* mind, everything is both fantasy and real. According to experts it is up to the particular culture to define reality. Phenomena such as superstitions, folk beliefs, and legends are merely expressed in the *social* narrative of a nation.

In most nations, the *social* narrative describes the Jews as more nefarious than non-Jews, more threatening and devil-like.

And the myth of the Jews' nefarious ways persists, in part, because it is consistent with the ongoing *social* narrative. For example, the fantasy that "Jews are rich" maintains social group envy and the fantasy of Jewish wealth through chicanery. The narrative does not mention that 25 percent of Jews reside below the poverty level. Still, this rumor persists where Jews are visibly poorer, or do not even reside.

But social hatred has never been about reality. It is about group perception and fear, threat, and power.

In the *social* mind, perception is everything. For instance, researchers find that perceptions of Jews are different than other groups. The Jews have the highest rates of "entitativity" (realness) and "essentialism" (biologically determined traits) compared to other ethnic groups (Kofta and Sedek 2005). Jews are perceived as more threatening than other groups and receive disproportionately more negative stereotypes. In most Western nations, hate crimes against Jews or their property are consistently highest. One early survey was particularly foretelling. As America was to about to enter World War II, ratings by *American Christian* of the top U.S. enemies listed Germans first, Japanese second, and the Jews third.

Alleged traits of the Jew are learned early on. The results of a potato chip study are telling. Polish school children were given three bags of potato chips—the first was marked Dutch, the next was marked Austrian, and the third was emblazoned with a Jewish Star of David. Children ate the chips and were asked which ones tasted better. Overwhelmingly, the claimed the Dutch chips tasted the best, followed by Austrian. According to the children, the least-tasty were the bags marked with Jewish labels. The chips in each bag were all the same (Czyzewka 1994).

Out of the mouths of babes and into college, not much has changed in terms of the imaginary Jew. University students expressed a belief that Jews were different than other ethnic groups. They were thought to be more determined and more negative than other ethnic groups. Although the original study was in 1936, similar questions were repeated in 2006, and Jewish traits were still viewed as permanent and threatening.

The results of an adult survey are also significant. Specifically, 19 percent had an "active" and 24 percent had a "passive" negative image of Jews. When the word "Jew" was introduced, it conjured up a folkloric image 43 percent of the time (Michlic, uncited survey 2006). Hebrew University's series on antisemitism has documented similar results in Japan, Romania, Poland, and Russia.

The ongoing social narrative is so powerful that it occurs and survives even in nations without any Jews at all.

"The disappearance of Jews within the society has not led to the disappearance of antisemitism, but rather to its abstraction through the emphasis on the mythical character of the Jew," Hebrew University's Leon Volovici noted.

He continued:

> In this new situation, the danger from Jews is perceived as an invisible, demonic conspiracy in which the concrete presence of Jews is no longer relevant or necessary ... An antisemitc element could be detected in public discourse, in culture, and in every manifestation expressing a state of mind, ideological orientation (and disorientation), and political options. Well-known stereotypes and myths were reproduced, and new ones forged.[1]

Myth and reality lines blur over and over. A study by Alyson Pendlebury (2005, 220) found a host of key antisemitc themes in British accounts of World War I, which resulted in at least one Jewish soldier's death at the hands of a Christian soldier because the victim might have been "a White Slave trafficker and a spy." More recently, the same indicting social myths were used by the Arab media to portray Jews as heartless, enemies of humanity, bloodthirsty, child-killers, and controllers of the world, except now it includes Nazism (Kotek 2004; Uriely 2006; and Wistrich 2005). And while criticism of the Israeli military may well be unrelated to antisemitism, it would not explain how statistically stereotyped beliefs of Jews are correlated with anti-Israeli sentiment (Baum and Naka-zwa 2007).

Antisemitc Legends

In antiquity, the Jews of Alexandria (1 BC) were rumored to worship donkey heads. Anticipating the thirteenth century blood libel rumors, Greeks were said to be kidnapped by Jews fattened for a year in the temple then ritually killed. Jews were thought to swear an oath of hostility to the Greeks.

By the Middle Ages, myths about Jews increased. Jews and the devil were now clearly linked. American historians Marvin Perry and Frederick Schweitzer contend that "people whose inherited folk memory viewed Jews as evil children of Satan and whose clergy often still propagated this myth" (2002, 260). Notes of the witches' "Sabbath" (Ginzburg 1991, 1), or as Elaine Pagels contends, a "Satanization" was forthcoming. Like the devil, Jews were thought to emit a foul odor (Dundes 1991).

According to European folklore of the Middle Ages, the Jew and the pig were so closely linked that in the fourteenth century, forced converts were called "marranos," Castilin for "pig." But it was the iconography of the Judensau that stood the test of time (*Judensau*, chapter 2). Throughout parts of Europe, butchers renamed the most succulent part of the pig the "damsel" or "Jewess." Parts of Germany created a cloven foot tax for Jewish visitors. In court, Jews were required to tell the truth while standing on the flayed skin of a sow or swearing on their mother's body. If found guilty, they were hung upside-down in the same manner in which a butcher slaughters a hog. Pig castrators in the Pyrenees adopted the uniform of the Jewish mohel (circumciser). Identifying a pig by cutting his ear soon transformed into cuts on Jew's ears and parodied by the antisemitc jeer "Here's your father's ear." Romans would roll an elderly Jew in a spike-lined barrel down Mt. Testaccio to welcome Easter. But by 1312, they decided to exchange the Jew for two pigs, which were placed in silk suits and driven in an elegant carriage to the mountaintop. Christian house painters in Germany would paint a pig on the walls of Jewish homes and cover it with a light layer of plaster. Eventually the plaster would wear away, revealing the Jews' "true nature."

Years later, Hitler would force Christian wives and fiancés of Jewish men to wear signs of sows. During the Spanish Inquisition and beyond, Jewish food such as the matzo ball was hunted out by sixteenth-century Roman Catholic priests who roamed the streets of Madrid sniffing for Jewish cookery. If found, one faced a future of conversion or death (Allen 2002).

The Jew's body was believed to be different than a Christian's. More primal and ape-like, but decrepit, "small, black, and hairy all over; his back is bent, his feet are flat; his eyes squint, and his lips smack; he has an evil smell, is promiscuous, and loves to deflower, impregnate, and infect blond girls." (*Mein Kampf* 1923). And in Romania, the Jews were thought of as big people with red hair and special powers (Oistenau 2001). Gender and anatomical differences were also rumored. Jewish men menstruated and were feminized. Indeed at the turn of the twentieth century in Austria, a women's clitoris was deemed "the Jew." Jewish women also were said to deliver children sideways, similar to pigs

Jewish youth were equally as culpable. The seed and virus of the Jew would quickly mature into adulthood. Spending any time with the Jew made one vulnerable their ways—a disease that was viral and like the devil, and could find a victim in the weak willed. Jewishness knew no bounds. One could also be accused of having thoughts that would undermine the social order—Jew-like openness to new ideas, such as liberalism, is an accusation routinely expressed in Polish and Russian politics.

Disease metaphors were not uncommon. A "contaminable social disease," the Jews were to be killed off, expelled, or contained in the social body. Containment took the form of Jew streets and Jew regions, such as Russia's Pale, France's Villejuif, India (Cochin), and England's Jew Town. Though more integrated in England, the Jews were still not to be trusted, and were for the most part separated from the rest of the populace and moved to ghettos. The first ghettoes opened in Genoa, Italy, in 1516, and later spread to Germany, Spain, and Portugal.

But it is the Jews' psychological makeup, their character flaw or nature as an "underminer," that seals their fate. All other uncomplimentary traits—treachery and seduction, for example—seem to follow from the key trait.

Deicide and Poisoners of the Prophet

Table 1 offers a way of conceptualizing the key components of antisemitc folklore. Jews are widely believed to have killed the son/God of Christianity and the Prophet of Islam, and refused to convert. After murdering both major religions' most-revered leaders, the Jew was presumed guilty and was to be punished. The Jew was anti-God and, by extension, anti-country and anti-nature.

What kind of people could kill God or his prophet? It could only be those sent by the antichrist or Satan himself. The folkloric Jew became the devil incarnate. As the devil's disciples, Jews were perceived a sorcerers or magicians, able to work magic against the Christian community. This belief served as the basis for the charge that the Jewish population desecrated the host and committed acts of ritual murder on the innocents (e.g., vulnerable Christian children). It is thought that some Jews did engage in magic, but the magic was based on the power of good/God.[2]

Table 1: Antisemitc Legend Themes

THEME	*SOURCE*	*MYTHOLOGY*
1. UNDERMINES GOD		
devil/antichrist	New Testament (Judas, deicide)	Host desecration/blood libel
black magic	Koran (poison prophet)	
2. UNDERMINES SOCIETY		
Conspiracy	Bible	
		Poisoners (wells)
Money	Moneylenders	Against "The People/State
Special status	Politics: Jewish lobby	Sinister cabal Elders of Zion/
		Neo-con lobby
		Liberalism
3. UNDERMINES SOCIAL ORDER		
		Disease carriers/contaminators
Jewish	In the blood (limpieza de sangre)	The Plague
	Mental/phys ill	
blood		Foetor Judaicus, men = men-
		struate
	Contain Convert or Kill	

After the deicide and poisoning accusations, Jews were pariahs and universal underminers who were capable of supernatural crime. Especially for Christians, the Passion is the center point of the religion, and the culpability is clearly set upon the Jews. By comparison, Pontius Pilate and the Romans are exonerated as Pilate "washes his hands," but Jews never apologize and convert, so their fate is sealed for the rest of time—"let his blood be on us and our children" (Matthew 27:25). Reality or fantasy matters not.

The tale of poisoning the Prophet by a Jewess goes something like this: Immediately following the conquest of Kheybar (a Jewish date farm region), a Jewish women prepared a dinner for Muhammad and some of his men. Unknown to the Muslims, she had put poison into the lamb or goat that was served at dinner. Muhammad ate some of the poisoned lamb and died from it three years later.

Toxicology limits notwithstanding, and the unlikeliest of death from food poisoning three years after the fact, makes no difference in fantasy. Yet for some reason, poisoning of the Prophet never attains the status in Islamic antisemitism as it does in Christianity's antisemitism. More indicting is the Jews' refusal to convert to Islam—Jewish insubordination and stubbornness for refusing to adapt to Islam's ways. All serve to create a narrative of the Jews as enemies of the state and as with Christianity, underminers of all that is good and godly.

Subsequently, several spin-off legends have emerged that are now secular and permit greater myth mobility. A pariah people (Maccoby 1996) with myths that could now serve as a warrant for genocide (Cohen 1996), the myths become detached from their religious wellsprings and moved into civic secular life, and socially transmitted into tales and jokes and rumor.

Eternal wanderers (eternally damned for shunning Jesus)
Ritual murderers of the innocent (murder of the Prophet and involved behind the scenes in Jesus' death)
Those who betray (Sanhedrin-based, Jewess poisoning of the Prophet)
To be retaliated (calls for his "blood be upon us and our children")
Host desecrators (symbolic repetition ritual murder)
Elders planning planetary takeover (Sanhedrin-based)
Money usurers (golden calf, temple money changers)
Moneylenders
Chimeras (not human/inferior/supernatural)

The Bible's Sanhedrin may have served as the model for Jewish conspiracy themes, which lied dormant until the nineteenth century and the publication of the Protocols of the Elders of Zion.

Less likely than anyone to benefit from the prevailing social order, Jews were regarded as treasonous, unpatriotic, and prone to undermine through their liberalism and universal thinking. Today many of those politics can be seen in the Arab news media, projected onto Israel and the secret Jewish cabals within the United States that force the hand of power.

Not only do Jews undermine God and society and the State, they undermine the racial hierarchy and are immutable. It is "in the blood" as the Spanish Inquisition's *limpeiza* laws had declared. Jews cannot be anything other than a Jew. *The Eternal Jew, The Operated Jew* and The Poison Mushroom's *Why Do Jews get Baptized?* each fashion an answer: like leopard's spots, Jews can change their appearance, but not their traits inside.

A popular Romanian tale demonstrates the dehumanization: "Ion, who did you chance on the road? Answer: A man and a Jew."[3] Similarly, Joshua Trachtenberg recounted a story of a friend who visited a small town in Quebec where children remarked, "Oh look a Jew." Another said, "It is not a Jew, but a man." His colleague reported the same experience in South Africa "Dit is geen mens, dit is een Jude" (Trachtenberg 1966/1983, xiv). Then again, journalists and academics address Christian and Jewish relations as "Poles and Jews" or "Germans and Jews," as if Jews were not citizens of those nations. Former French Prime Minister Raymond Barre's response to a 1980 Palestinian bombing of a Paris synagogue said it all: "This appalling attack was intended to hit Jews on their way to the synagogue ... it has hit *innocent French people* who happened to be in the Rue Copernic." (emphasis added). Clearly, the Jewish citizenry of France were never believed to be sufficiently innocent—or French.

The Jews' essence can be likened to an alien in a science fiction movie—one who will strike at you at a moment's notice.

"He was a creature of a different order," wrote Hebrew University Historian Robert Wistrich. "Not really human, at least not in the sense that Christians were (1999, 4). The Jew was a chimera, the fire-breathing monster of Greek mythology consisting of the lion, goat, and snake. By definition, chimeras are fantasies, figments of the imagination, monsters that although dressed syntactically in the clothes of real humans have never been seen, and are projections of mental processes unconnected with the real people of the out-group (Langmuir 1990, 1992; Wistrich 1991; 1999). This chimerical fantasy has an antithetical relation to truth, not one of simple distortion," (Smith, 1996, 225) and encompasses an array of unconscious fears which creates the perfect enemy: a lurking, invisible force that waits in the wings ready to undermine all that is good, right, and true. This "extraordinary elastic abstraction" (Wistrich 1995) becomes a lightning rod for all that is feared and hated.[4]

Death by Legend

Folklorist Alan Dundes began to explain how people acted on a social myth. But it has been antisemitism researchers who have pointed to the relationship between folk beliefs and anti-Semitic attacks. Once one accepts the premise that most people are prone to believing what the culture tells them, and once one accepts that many of those people conform to social forces—then acting out socially unconscious directives is quite tenable (Baum, unpublished manuscript; Weinberg 2007).

Blood libels are sensationalized allegations that a specific person or group engages in human sacrifice, often accompanied by the claim that the blood of victims is used in various rituals and/or acts of cannibalism. The alleged victims are often children. Some accusations have included Christians, Cathars, Carthaginians, Knights Templar, witches, Christian heretics, Roma, Wiccans, Druids, neo-pagans, Native Americans, and Satanists. But the folk belief has persisted best against the Jews.

For instance, while the origins may have begun in antiquity, the rumor-legend was common by the Middle Ages. Even as late as the nineteenth century, as many as thirty blood libels had been circulating—the most famous one being the Damascus blood libel of 1840. In Damascus, a Capuchin monk was rumored to have disappeared through the nefarious ways of the Jews, who were said to have martyred him—murdered so Christian blood could be used for a Jewish meal, to be exact. Retributive justice by the Christian community soon claimed fifty-five Jewish children in exchange. However, no missing monk was ever found.

In Russia, a Kiev factory superintendent named Mendel Beiliss was tried in 1913 for "killing a Christian boy so the blood could be used in the unleavened bread," and after several trials was discontinued for lack of evidence. Others were not so lucky that year.

In Atlanta, pencil factory superintendent Leo Frank was accused of the rape and murder of a young employee named Mary Phagan, and was subsequently lynched and hanged outside the courthouse. Blood libel accusations subsided only to be awakened a few years later Massena, New York. There in 1928, on the eve of a holy day and ritual meal celebrating the Jews freedom from Egyptian pharaoh—Passover—the town's Jews were accused of kidnapping and killing a four-year-old girl. Police were called to investigate, and the girl was later found in a nearby woods. Similar rumors and accusations leading to police involvement had occurred in neighboring Clayton, Pennsylvania in 1913, and Fall River and Pittsfield, Massachusetts in 1919, as well as in Chicago that same year (Perry and Schweitzer 2002).

White slavery allegations and blood libel accusations are quite similar.

"Each involves violence to a defenseless young person and the projection of hate onto a symbolic substitute for the evil father. White slavery was the sexualization of the blood libel," noted folklorist Veronique Campion-Vincent.

The two themes transferred all to well to Orleans, France, in 1969. While the rest of the world was tuning in and dropping out, Jewish dress shop proprietors were fending off allegations that they had been kidnapping local Catholic girls for the underground slave trade. The authorities were brought in to investigate and found no supporting evidence—which led the town folk to believe the police had merely been "bought off by the Jews." A bishop great authority was called in to dispel the rumor, and only then did the allegations and threats aimed at Orleans' Jewish families cease.

Be it Bury Saint Edmunds, England, in 1190, or the front page of an Arab newspaper in the new millennium, the blood libel myth enjoys a social life unmatched by other antisemitc fables.

Yet the blood libel myth is hardly the only viable antisemitc rumor. Holocaust denial recently served as a model for the reverse—reality made into a legend.

"One way of showing what stories reveal about cultural prejudices is to turn those stories against the storytellers," observed James Shapiro in *Shakespeare and the Jews.* (Columbia University Press, 1995). So, when Eric Hunt, 22 attacked Holocaust scholar Elie Wiesel on February 1, 2007, in San Francisco, he posted the following on his Web site:

> I had planned on … getting Wiesel into my custody, with a cornered Wiesel finally forced to state the truth on videotape … exposing the "Pope of the Holocaust religion" for being nothing but a genocidal liar.

Social Transmission of Antisemitic Myths

Understanding the social transmission of such legends is fairly simple. From psychology research of superstition, rumor, and legend, we know that transmission and "stickiness" of an idea is due to the three C's: concise, consistent, and crazy—emotionally unnerving and threatening. And it's especially effective if someone in authority has endorsed the rumor as well. Experts believe that a story that tingles the imagination has the faster transmission, albeit certainly not the most accurate transmission. The transmission is considerably quicker if the tale is one that fits in with an ongoing narrative—in this case, the ongoing tale of the perceived undermining ways of Jews.

Historian Raul Hilberg has noted that there was virtually no antisemitism among the Amazonian Indian tribes. After Christian missionaries exposed the population to certain biblical passages, the tribes were vigilant, ready for the menacing tribe known as the Jews. Romanian diarist Mihail Sebastian documented the ease of folklore transmission.

> In the middle of five or six passersby, I glimpsed the poor madman who once used to wander with a switch and whistle from one streetcar to the next, giving imaginary signals for it to stop or start.

Well, that stuttering half-wit was telling how "a yid woman fired with a revolver last night from the roof of that building over there—and a trooper was hit."

"A yid woman you say?" asked an elderly gentleman, quite well dressed, quite unruffled.

"Yeah, one of them yid bitches!"

"And didn't they do anything to her?"

"You bet they did. They arrested her, took her away."

I looked closely at the people listening. No one had the least doubt about the truth of this absurd story.… Did they not know that the soldier fell in a real street battle in which hundreds of bullets were fired? But what was the point of asking? Who would have listened? Isn't it easier and quicker to believe what others tell you? "A yid woman opened fire."[5]

The Jews' reputation had always preceded them. Their presence carried a warning label. Historically, Jews had been depicted in theological polemics, sermons, mystery plays, fiction, and the visual arts as representing mysterious fearsome and evil forces (Trachtenberg 1996). From there, it is not difficult to understand how other sinister and political tales evolved. In Mihail Sebastian's records, his former friend, the poet Mircea, writes:

The Poles' resistance in Warsaw is a Jewish resistance. Only yids are capable of blackmail of putting women and children in the front line to take advantage of the Germans' sense of scruple. Rather than a Romania again invaded by kikes, it would be better to have a German protectorate.[6]

Social Myth Mindedness

People believe folklore more than fact. They link it to intuition and resist giving it up. It is revealing that 90 percent of American newspapers contain daily horoscopes, but fewer than 10 percent offer science columns.

"We know more about our automobiles than our minds," quipped Pulitzer Prize winning scientist E.O. Wilson. He is right. We spend most of our waking time in fantasy. By one estimate, illogical beliefs may occupy the vast majority of human thoughts.[7] The chart below indicates total percentages of those polled who believe in the following supernatural phenomena:

<u>Mythical Nation:</u>

UFOs (polls range from 40% to 53%)
Ghosts (polls range from 35% to 39%)
Astrology (polls range from 41 to 52%)
ESP (66%)
Ability to communicate with the dead (25%)
Lost continent of Atlantis (33%)
Which best predicts the future? Bible (49%) Old Farmer's Almanac (22%) Psychics (16%)

"I know perfectly well that in the scientific sense, there is no such thing as race," Hitler once told a friend (Montagu 1997). It did not matter. He knew the rest of the world believed the folk theory of race. People project the folkloric Jews onto the real ones and seal their beliefs with pseudo-race theory—a folk theory that has been called "man's most dangerous myth." (Montagu 1997) Wholly unsupported by science, race theory continues as the most popular explanation of ethnic group behavior in the world. Philosopher Ernst Cassirer wrote:

> When we first heard of the political myths, we found them so absurd and incongruous, so fantastic and ludicrous, that we could hardly be prevailed upon to take them seriously. By the end of the war, however, it had become clear to all of us that this was a great mistake.… The mythical monsters were not entirely destroyed. They were used for the creation of a new universe and they still survive in this universe.

Princeton University's Jan T. Gross estimated that 500 and 1,500 antisemitc killings took place in postwar Poland in 1945–46. He observed that a new set of social myths emerged that linked the imaginary Jew to Communists.

> That many people believed in both—many of the same people, one might add—and that many people acted on these believes, unfortunately does make them "real in their consequences." But it does not make them true. Jews were not drinking Christian blood, just as they were not using it in their rituals, and Jews were not responsible for bringing communism to Poland. In other words, that Jews were communist or that Jews were vampires could not have been the reason they were perceived as a threat by their neighbors—because they were neither. (Gross 2006, 246)

He later concluded that it could not be possible for so many to believe such a crazy idea as a blood libel, or any of the myths, and proceeded to err on the side of logic, not appreciating the social transmission of the imaginary Jew.

"We must seek," Gross said, "the reasons for the novel, virulent quality of postwar antisemitism in Poland, not in collective hallucinations nor in prewar attitudes, but in actual experiences acquired during the war years." (Gross 2006, 246)

Gross searches for explanations—economic competition, opportunistic motives, etc.—and tries to forget that antisemitism occurs among the rich as well as the poor. He doesn't want to remember that antisemitism exists in nations devoid of actual Jews. He does not want to accept the linkage of bizarre social rumors accompanying pogroms. He does not know that most people are not mentally healthy or mature in their beliefs (Kessler, et al., 2006).

So who needs Wannsee when fantasy and fear coupled with rumor and myth can create such a vibrant evil as The Jews. Perhaps Dr. Gross was trying to make sense of the litany of senseless antisemitc deaths. Perhaps he was hoping that the horrors perpetrated could not have been triggered by something as trite as an unfounded rumor. Perhaps he was wishing people were not delusional when it came to beliefs about the Jews.

But they are. Just how many people believe in the imaginary Jew? While we do not have exact figures, the best estimates can be gleaned from antisemitism survey research. Parenthetically, the psychometric properties of tests used to determine antisemitism are also revealing. Antisemitism rated as higher or lower is determined based on the number of imaginary Jew statements a person endorses and the strength of those myth beliefs. An example is provided below.

Antisemitc Belief Scale

Jews have lot of irritating faults.
Jews stick together too much.
Jews don't care what happens to anyone else.
Jews like to head things.
Jews use shady practices.
Jews have too much power/business power.

The transmission of the imaginary Jew keeps surveys well-nourished. Among the most-Westernized nations, anti-Semitism rates range between 20 and 40 percent. These rates double or triple in Islamic nations.[8]

Political scientist Daniel Goldhagen observed:

> The evidence that so many ordinary people did maintain at the center of their world view palpably absurd beliefs about Jews like those of Hitler articulated in *Mein Kampf* is overwhelming.... [They were] animated by the beliefs about Jews that made them willing to become consenting mass executioners. (1996, 455)

Antisemitism Surveys

USA	20%
Britain	24%
France	33%
Germany	36%
Spain	45%
Russia	50%
Turkey	89%
Pakistan	98%
Morocco	98%

Survey not permitted in Jordan (Pew Global Attitudes, 2006)
http://pewglobal.org/reports/display.php?ReportID=206

While some aspects of Goldhagen's tenet have been taken to task, few can argue against the persistence and voraciousness of the history of antisemitism—a history based on myth, rumor, and superstition.

2

Antisemitic Lore by Culture and Country

The greatest enemy of truth is very often not the lie, deliberate, contrived and dishonest, but the myth—persistent, persuasive and unrealistic.
    —John F. Kennedy

Brothers Jacob and Wilhelm Grimm began collecting common folktales and peasant lore and altering them to emphasize cultural values and social mores. Revising many peasant tales to teach the lessons of "German character"—ordung, fleiss and sparsamkeit (order, diligence, and thriftiness)—the Brothers Grimm portrayed all things non-German as wasteful, sloppy, and lazy. Kamenetsky (1992) and later Lipson (2001) assessed the moral and social content of Grimm's Brothers *The Jew In The Thorns* (Jew as a thief) *The Good Bargain* (A Jew lies and deceives regarding money) and in the somewhat positive *The Sun Will Bring It to Light*. (Christian kills a Jew and almost gets away with it) The tales themes contain values that favor poverty over wealth, peasants over "outsiders," and rewards through violence.

Folklorist Jack Zipes further notes that the Grimms' Germanic hero always triumphs over the undeserving namely those of power and privilege. These depictions, showcased in such antisemitc tales as *The Good Bargain*, served as powerful transmitters of cultural mores. Several themes rejuvenated in Nazi folklore a century later.

What is the fallout from antisemitic folklore? In *Race Attitudes in Children (1929)*, British sociologist Bruno Lasker recounts his experience,

> The word Jew always awakens in my mind a momentary feeling of unpleasantness. I have never had any experience with a Jew which would arouse this feeling and I was unable to account for it until I remembered a fairy tale which somebody read to me when I was small. In this story, the villain is a Jew, lying, thieving and altogether a despicable character. The story must have made a deep impression on me: as I had never seen a Jew, my childish mind pictured them all like this one (Newall, 1973 p.97).

The medieval Jew was believed to have horns and a tail and to be related to the Devil himself. In the seventeenth century, Sir Thomas Browne gave it as a 'received opinion' that Jews had a special and distinctive smell, but says that he does not believe it. By 1936, the Nazis had transformed odor to vision. At the time, the newspaper *Der Sturmer* warned readers that "a bull can simply by catching sight of a Jew, become mad." (Burstein, 1959 p.365)

Unfortunately early antisemitic learning may be enduring. When psychoanalyst Morton Ostow (1996) and his fellow analysts examined their Christian analysands, they found that most of the patient had negative associations to Jews. Not only did some recall coloring pictures of the deicide, but also of stories and folktales they had heard.

Antisemitic folktales are not the only source of antisemitic sentiment, but they do seem consistent and prevalent. The table below offers a brief overview of the myths involved in the estimated 400,000 antisemitic deaths (pre-Holocaust) the Holocaust's six million and the daily attacks on Jews globally since that time.

The common denominator for all antisemitic myths is the role of the Jew as an *underminer*. Jews undermine Christianity, the social/natural order and are chimerical.

Undermining Jew as …	Folk Tale
1 Anti-Christian	
(Deicide)	Bloody Children of Jews (Ger) Judgment Day(EE) The Lost Jew (Ger)
	Battadeu (It) Malchus at the Column (It) Judas (Bible)
	Chapel of the Holy Body at Magdenburg (Ger)
(Ritual Murder/Blood Libel)	Jews Stone (Aus/Ger) Girl Killed by the Jews (Ger)
	Bloody Children of the Jews, Imprisoned Jew at Magdeburg (Ger)
(Wanderers)	Eternal Jew on the Matterhorn (Swiss)
2 Anti-Society	Jew as Devil (Arabic) Poison Mushroom (N)
	What is the Talmud? (N) Judas, Protocols Elders Zion(R)
3 Anti-Human/Chimera	How the Jews came to be Among Us?(N) The Operated Jew(Ger)
	Pferrkorn (Ger); Why do the Jews Get Baptized? (N)
	Why the Jews do not Eat Pork?(Rom)
(Physically Different)	How to Recognize a Jew (N); How Jews Got Freckles (Rom)
	Apes & Pigs (Ar); Hyenas (Ethiopia) Judensau (Ger)
Traits	
Magical	Sun will bring it to light. (Ger)
Rainmakers	(EE) (Sp)
Treacheous	Judas; Expulsion of the Jews from Prussia (Ger)
Parvenu	Poem (Puck)
Thief/Money	Youtai (China) Jew in the Bush/Thorns (Ger)
	The Good Bargain (Ger) Oisin in Tir N n og (Ir)
	How a German Farmer was Driven (Ger)

Key: Ar (Arabic) N=Nazi Germany; It=Italy; Ger=Germany; Ir=Irelad; R=Russia; Sp=Spain EE=Eastern Europ

Arab Culture (Medieval)

Antisemitic folk tales in medieval Arab and Islam is comparatively neutral with both positive and negative portraits of Jews. Portrayals of Jews in the Arabian Nights are clearly positive though Yoel Yosef Rivlin has documented that in earlier versions of Aladdin, the protagonist is cheated by a Jew and saved by a Muslim competitor. Christian Arabs are not immune from antisemitic folklore as well.

The Virgin Mary and the Plowmen (Palestinian)

When the Virgin Mary peace be on her was on the flight to Egypt with her son in her arms, she passed by some plowmen making furrows in their field. She said to them, "Though today you're only sowing before the sun rises tomorrow morning your field will be ready to harvest. But remember, if anyone comes this way and asks about me, say "she was here just as we were getting ready to plant these chick-peas." Indeed when the Beni Israil (Jews) who were after the Virgin came to the place on the very next day these same plowmen were busy harvesting chick peas. The Beni Israil asked, "Has a woman carrying a child passed your way presently? The plowman replied "By God such a one did go by but that was when we were digging the furrow to sow this crop. "Oh ho' said her pursuers 'that must have been some time ago. How will we catch up with her now? [1]

The Mountain That Moved (Coptic)

According to the Coptic legend Caliph Al-Muizz, a generally enlightened man, enjoyed a good debate, and one day in the year 979 he invited Pope Abram and Anba Sawiris, Bishop of Ashmenein, together with a Jew (Vizier/Minister to the Caliph) named Jacob Ibn Killis, to a meeting. A few insults flowed, but Anba Sawiris got the better of the argument. Ibn Killis planned revenge. (in other versions, it is written "Naturally [this was] the advice of a Jew for they have hated Copts all their lives" (see El-Shamy, 1980 p. 168) He told the Caliph that Jesus had said: "If one has faith only as small as a mustard seed, one can say to a mountain, 'Move!' and it will move for you." "If they can't move a mountain," Ibn Killis pointed out, "Christianity is not a pure religion," according to the legend. The Caliph thought this was a golden opportunity to move the end of the Muqattam Hill which was spoiling his view, and therewith ordered the Pope either to move the mountain, or concede it could not be done. The Pope asked for three days' grace, and the Christian community—which at that time would have been about 50 per cent of the population—held a fast (Copts still add an extra three days of fasting to their 40-day Christmas fast in memory of this event). After praying for the three days, the Pope enlisted the help of the saintly (shoemaker) Samaan the Tanner. The Copts assembled on one side of the mountain and the Muslims and Jews on the other. The Christians prayed fervently and the Pope, guided by Samaan, waved his staff, and as they prayed the earth shook with a huge earthquake which toppled the hill. There was panic: buildings could be seen falling and the Caliph begged the Pope to put a stop to the tremor. When calm had returned St .Samaan was nowhere to be found, and to this day a saying goes: "Go, like Samaan, and never come back." In other versions the cobbler ordered the mountain to fall on him so he would not be famous. The Jewish Vizier is shot or imprisoned for his treachery (El-Shamy, 1980). [2]

According to Indiana University folklorist Hasan El-Shamy, the Jew is depicted negatively as are other religions at times. The Jew doing something nefarious or undermining is certain e.g Motif K2287.3S [3]

Emmanuel Sivan's (1985), analysis revealed a pattern of five stereotypic images of the Jew in Algerian folklore. As expressed in popular literature, jokes, songs, and satire, Jews appear as: barbaric, impoverished, filthy, dishonest, and lecherous. With French emancipation in 1870, Algerian Spanish, Italian and Maltese immigrants became antisemitic as well. It appears that antisemitic folklore in Muslim culture was more ambivalent than that of Christendom. Some antisemitic folklore was Hadith or Koranic based. Several examples from the Koran follow:

> According to Islam, the ancient Jews were turned into animals for transgressing the word of God. This divine punishment is mentioned in the most important sources of Islamic religious law, in both the Koran's recounting of the divine revelation, and in Hadith the interpretation by ninth-century sages and Al-Bukhari which mention also mice, lizards, and other animals in the same context. The divine punishment of Jews is mentioned in three Koranic verses: "... They are those whom Allah has cast aside and on whom His wrath has fallen and of whom He has made some as apes and swine ..." (5:60); "... You have surely known the end of those from amongst you who transgressed in the matter of the Sabbath, in consequence of which we condemned them: Be ye like apes, despised" (2:65)and "when, instead of amending, they became more persistent in the pursuit of that which they were forbidden, we condemned them: Be ye as apes, despised" (7:166) [4]

The Jew portrayed as ape is transferred into legend as depicted in Khalifah, the Fisherman of Baghdad. (abridged)

There was once in tides of yore and in ages and times long gone before in the city of Baghdad a fisherman, Khalifah hight, a pauper wight, who had never once been married in all his days. It chanced one morning that he took his net and went with it to the river as was his wont, with the view of fishing before the others came. When he reached the bank, he girt himself and tucked up his skirts. Then stepping into the water, he spread his net and cast it a first cast and a second, but it brought up naught. He ceased not to throw it till he had made ten casts, and still naught came up therein, wherefore his breast was straitened and his mind perplexed concerning his case and he said: "I crave pardon of God the Great, there is no god but He, the Living, the Eternal, and unto Him I repent. There is no Majesty and there is no Might save in Allah, the Glorious, the Great! Whatso He willeth is and whatso He nilleth is not! Upon Allah (to Whom belong Honor and Glory!) dependeth daily bread! Now when Khalifah had made an end of his verse, he went down to the river, and casting his net, waited awhile. After which he drew it up and found therein a fine young fish, with a big head, a tail like a ladle, and eyes like two gold pieces. When Khalifah saw this fish, he rejoiced, for he had never in his life caught its like, so he took it, marveling, and carried it to the ape of Abu al-Sa'adat the Jew, as 'twere he had gotten possession of the universal world. Quoth the ape, "O Khalifah, what wilt thou do with this, and with thine ape?" and quoth the fisherman: "I will tell thee, O monarch of monkeys, all I am about to do. Know then that first, I will cast about to make away with yonder accursed, my ape, and take thee in his stead, and give thee every day to eat of whatso thou wilt ... And the Jew said, "Meseemeth thou wouldst have me become a Moslem." Khalifah rejoined: "By Allah, O Jew, an thou Islamize, 'twill nor advantage the Moslems nor damage the Jews. And in like manner, an thou hold to thy misbelief 'twill nor damage the Moslems nor advantage the Jews. But what I desire of thee is that thou rise to thy feet and say: 'Bear witness against me, O people of the market, that I barter my ape for the ape of Khalifah the fisherman and my lot in the world for his lot and my luck for his luck'." Quoth the Jew, "If this be all thou desirest, 'twill sit lightly upon me." So he rose without stay or delay and standing on his feet, repeated the required words. After which he turned to the fisherman and asked him, "Hast thou aught else to ask of me?" "No," answered he, and the Jew said, "Go in peace!"

Koranic/Hadith quotes:

1.   They used to fabricate things and falsely ascribe them to Allah. Allah Almighty says: "That is because they say: We have no duty to the Gentiles. They speak a lie concerning Allah knowingly." (Al-'Imran:75) Also: "The Jews say: Allah's hand is fettered. Their hands are fettered and they are accursed for saying so. Nay, but both His hands are spread out wide in bounty. He bestoweth as He will." (Al-Ma'idah:64) In another verse

Almighty Allah says: "Verily Allah heard the saying of those who said, (when asked for contributions to the war): "Allah, forsooth, is poor, and we are rich! We shall record their saying with their slaying of the Prophets wrongfully and We shall say: Taste ye the punishment of burning!" (Al-`Imran:181)

2.   They love to listen to lies. Concerning this Allah says: "and of the Jews: listeners for the sake of falsehood, listeners on behalf of other folk" (Al-Ma'idah: 41)

3.   Disobeying Almighty Allah and never observing His commands. Allah says: "And because of their breaking their covenant, We have cursed them and made hard their hearts." (Al-Ma'idah: 13)

4.   Disputing and quarreling. This is clear in the verse that reads: "Their Prophet said unto them: Lo! Allah hath raised up Saul to be a king for you. They said: How can he have kingdom over us when we are more deserving of the kingdom than he is, since he hath not been given wealth enough?" (Al-Baqarah: 247)

5.   Hiding the truth and standing for misleading. This can be understood from the verse that reads: "… distort the Scripture with their tongues, that ye may think that what they say is from the Scripture, when it is not from the Scripture." (Al-`Imran: 78)

6.   Staging rebellion against the Prophets and rejecting their guidance. This is clear in the verse: "And when ye said: O Moses! We will not believe in thee till we see Allah plainly." (Al-Baqarah: 55)

7.   Hypocrisy. In a verse, we read: "And when they fall in with those who believe, they say: We believe; but when they go apart to their devils they declare: Lo! we are with you; verily we did but mock." (Al-Baqarah: 14) In another verse, we read: "Enjoin ye righteousness upon mankind while ye yourselves forget (to practice it)? And ye are readers of the Scripture! Have ye then no sense?" (Al-Baqarah: 44)

8.   Giving preference to their own interests over the rulings of religion and the dictates of truth. Allah says: "… when there cometh unto you a messenger (from Allah) with that which ye yourselves desire not, ye grow arrogant, and some ye disbelieve and some ye slay?" (Al-Baqarah: 87)

9.   Wishing evil for people and trying to mislead them. This is clear in the verse that reads: "Many of the People of the Scripture long to make you disbelievers after your belief, through envy on their own account, after the truth hath become manifest unto them." (Al-Baqarah: 109)

10. They feel pain to see others in happiness and are gleeful when others are afflicted with a calamity. This is clear in the verse that reads: "If a lucky chance befall you, it is evil unto them, and if disaster strike you they rejoice thereat." (Al-'Imran:120)

11. They are known of their arrogance and haughtiness. They claimed to be the sons and of Allah and His beloved ones. Allah tells us about this in the verse that reads: "The Jews and Christians say: We are sons of Allah and His loved ones." (Al-Ma'idah: 18)

12. Utilitarianism and opportunism are among their innate traits. This is clear in the verse that reads: "And of their taking usury when they were forbidden it, and of their devouring people's wealth by false pretences." (An-Nisa': 161)

13. Their impoliteness and indecent way of speech is beyond description. Referring to this, the Qur'anic verse reads: "Some of those who are Jews change words from their context and say: "We hear and disobey; hear thou as one who heareth not" and "Listen to us!" distorting with their tongues and slandering religion. If they had said: "We hear and we obey; hear thou, and look at us" it had been better for them, and more upright. But Allah hath cursed them for their disbelief, so they believe not, save a few." (An-Nisa':46)

14. It is easy for them to slay people and kill innocents. Nothing in the world is dear to their hearts than shedding blood and murdering human beings. They never give up this trait even with the Messengers and the Prophets. Allah says: "... and slew the prophets wrongfully." (Al-Baqarah: 61)

15. They are merciless and heartless. In this meaning, the Qur'anic verse explains: "Then, even after that, your hearts were hardened and became as rocks, or worse than rocks, for hardness." (Al-Baqarah: 74)

16. They never keep their promises or fulfill their words. Almighty Allah says: "Is it ever so that when ye make a covenant a party of you set it aside? The truth is, most of them believe not." (Al-Baqarah: 100)

17. They rush hurriedly to sins and compete in transgression. Allah says: "They restrained not one another from the wickedness they did. Verily evil was that they used to do!" (Al-MA'idah:79)

18. Cowardice and their love for this worldly life are their undisputable traits. To this, the Qur'an refers when saying: "Ye are more awful as a fear in their bosoms than Allah. That is because they are a folk who understand not. They will not fight against you in a body save in fortified villages or from behind walls. Their adversity among themselves is very

great. Ye think of them as a whole whereas their hearts are divers." (Al-Hashr:13–14) Allah Almighty also says: "And thou wilt find them greediest of mankind for life and (greedier) than the idolaters." (Al-Baqarah:96)

19. Miserliness runs deep in their hearts. Describing this, the Qur'an states: "Or have they even a share in the Sovereignty? Then in that case, they would not give mankind even the speck on a date stone." (An-Nisa':53)

20. 20. Distorting Divine Revelation and Allah's Sacred Books. Allah says in this regard: "Therefore woe be unto those who write the Scripture with their hands anthem say, "This is from Allah," that they may purchase a small gain therewith. Woe unto them for that their hands have written, and woe unto them for that they earn thereby." (Al-Baqara: 79) [5]

Hadith 4:626

Once while a Jew was selling something, he was offered a price that he was not pleased with. So, he said, "No, by Him Who gave Moses superiority over all human beings!" Hearing him, an Ansari man got up and slapped him on the face and said, "You say: By Him Who Gave Moses superiority over all human beings although the Prophet (Muhammad) is present amongst us!" The Jew went to the Prophet and said, "O Abu-l-Qasim! I am under the assurance and contract of security, so what right does so-and-so have to slap me?" The Prophet asked the other, "Why have you slapped". He told him the whole story. The Prophet became angry, till anger appeared on his face, and said, "Don't give superiority to any prophet amongst Allah's Prophets, for when the trumpet will be blown, everyone on the earth and in the heavens will become unconscious except those whom Allah will exempt. The trumpet will be blown for the second time and I will be the first to be resurrected to see Moses holding Allah's Throne. I will not know whether the unconsciousness which Moses received on the Day of Tur has been sufficient for him, or has he got up before me. And I do not say that there is anybody who is better than Yunus bin Matta."

Hadith 4:9

A Jew crushed the head of a girl between two stones. She was asked, "Who has done so to you, so-and-so? So-and-so?" Till the name of the Jew was mentioned, whereupon she nodded (in agreement). So the Jew was brought and was questioned till he confessed. The Prophet then ordered that his head be crushed with stones.

Hadith 4:620

> A Muslim and a Jew quarreled. The Muslim taking an oath, said, "By Him
> Who has preferred Muhammad over all people …!" The Jew said, "By Him
> Who has preferred Moses, over all people." The Muslim raised his hand and
> slapped the Jew who came to the Prophet to tell him what had happened
> between him and the Muslim. The Prophet said, "Don't give me superiority
> over Moses, for the people will become unconscious (on the Day of Resurrec-
> tion) and I will be the first to gain consciousness to see Moses standing and
> holding a side of Allah's Throne. I will not know if he has been among those
> people who have become unconscious; and that he has gained consciousness
> before me, or he has been amongst those whom Allah has exempted."

Hadith 3:849

> A Jew from Hira asked me which one of the two periods Musa (i.e. Prophet
> Moses) completed. I said, "I don't know, (but wait) till I see the most learned
> 'Arab and enquire him about it." So, I went to Ibn 'Abbas and asked him. He
> replied, "Moses completed the longer and better period." Ibn 'Abbas added,
> "No doubt, an apostle of Allah always does what he says."

Arab Culture (Post-1948)

While there is an established pattern of Arab antisemitic folklore, for the most
part, it paled in comparison to its Christian counterpart. Since the birth of the
State of Israel (1948) antisemitic/anti-Israeli folklore has proliferated and pervades all aspects of Arab and most Muslim culture.

There are multiple narratives demonstrating Arab victimization and blaming
Jews or Christians, the most recent being the conspiracy theory of 9–11. Where
minimization or flat out denial isn't employed, even the Holocaust has a remarkable twist. Historian Robert Satloff (Among the Righteous, Public Affairs, 2006)
notes that in the minds of many Arabs, the murder of six million Jews is history's
perverse revenge upon the Arabs. Christians may have crucified Jews but the
Christians expatiated their guilt by creating Israel. Consequently, the real suffering is by Arabs because land was stolen. Arabs continue to suffer in their homeland, generation after generation.

Nazi like antisemitic tales and anti-Israeli sentiment pervades Arab media bias-
ing the academy in the West (see Manfred Gestenteld's Academics Against Israel
and the Jews, JCPA, 2008) and Western media in general (see Bernard Harrison's
The Resurgence of Anti-Semitism, Rowman & Littlefield, 2006). The latest foray

against The Jews includes student textbooks and children's fairy tales. Some of the antisemitic folklore has found its way onto children's websites e.g.Yahoo's awladnaa.net. Clicking onto the banner one can read the following:

Did You Know?
—*Jews slaughtered 25 prophets of Allah and ritually kill children.*
—*Jews are responsible for all the world's corruption and deviance*
—*Jews who now occupy Palestine plan to take over the entire Middle East*

Satellite television broadcasts include *Horseman without a Horse*, a 41-part serialized version of the *Protocols of the Elders of Zion* (home video versions available online or in Arab video stores throughout Europe and North America). In the last decade, blood libel dramas and themes are televised regularly as far as Belarus (1997). Media watchgroups such as Honest Reporting, Memri and Mid-East Truth, monitor the broadcasts regularly. The following is an excerpt from a popular Abu Dhabi broadcast with then Prime Minister Sharon in the role of arch villain. [6]

Scene: In Dracula's "house." Dracula emerges from one of the coffins in the room.

Sharon: Dracula, my friend? (repeat) Dracula, my friend, it's me—Sharon. I've arrived. Here you go, my friend. (Hands Dracula a wine bottle, filled with blood)

Dracula: I'm not going to drink even one drop. Why is it that you use my name and profit behind my back? I, who sucks the blood of the world. How dare you come and suck my blood?

S: Dracula, my friend, this is not intentional.

D: What do you bring?

S: A bottle containing Arab blood for you to drink.

D: I don't drink out of a bottle. I don't drink blood that I don't know, Sharon.

S: What do you drink?

D: I want a present from you.

S: What present? Just name it, I am at your service.

D: I want warm blood that runs in veins.

S: No, No, I … Dracula!

Dracula bites Sharon in the neck.

New Scene: Newscaster: Here are the news. Dracula, the international vampire, was found dead after he was poisoned by sucking dirty blood, cold and filthy. The terrorist Sharon claimed responsibility.

Cartoons are a particularly effective means of propaganda in low literacy cultures. Belgium political scientist Joel Kotek (2004) has analyzed Arab cartoons, which routinely depict the Jew as devil and the ritual murder of children. "The main recurrent theme in these cartoons is 'the devilish Jew.' By extension, this image suggests that the Jewish religion must be diabolic, and the entire Jewish people evil. One Greek Orthodox cartoonist of Lebanese origin, conveys the message that the Jewish religion has caused the State of Israel to be so 'evil.' The cartoons link Jews and Nazis, leading readers to conclude that the only logical solution is their elimination. [7] Others examples include a glorification of suicide bombing. It is all formidable. As Lebanese Christian Brigitte Gabriel, author of *Because They Hate* (St. Martins, 2006) is quick to remind us, even the Nazis knew better than to use their children as human bombs.

The Jew as Devil

The above cartoon was spurred on by the 2,000 AD Papal visit to Israel and depicts the Pope saying 'peace on earth' while the Jew counters with colonies on earth. Content analysis of Arab cartoons reveals themes linking the Jew with: the deicide, Nazis, zoomorphism e.g. snakes, octopus, pigs monkeys, planetary take-over, corrupting force re: money, blood libel/ritual murders, infanticide, war-mongering and deserved recipients of suicide bombers. Arabic school textbooks suggest similar patterns of antisemitism (Stav, 2000).

Planetary Takeover by The Jew

The Jew as Nazi slaying of Arab innocents.

Armenia

It was a common belief among the Armenians that the Jews slaughter young Christian Armenians and use their blood at the Passover feast (see Blood Libel). In Amasya province, local Armenian priests and notables claimed that an Armenian woman had seen Jews slaughter a young Armenian boy and use his blood for religious purposes followed by the tortured confession and hanging of local Jews. The blood Libel occurred when Jewish merchants became too competitive or successful. At different times, the Turkish led genocide (1915) was said to be the handiwork of freemasons or The Jews.

Austria

The Jews Stone (see Blood Libel, Judenstein)

> In the year 1462 in the village of Rinn in Tyrol a number of Jews convinced a poor farmer to surrender his small child to them in return for a large sum of money. They took the child out into the woods, where, on a large stone, they martyred it to death in the most unspeakable manner. From that time the stone has been called the Jews' Stone. Afterward they hung the mutilated body on a birch tree not far from a bridge. The child's mother was working in a

field when the murder took place. She suddenly thought of her child, and without knowing why, she was overcome with fear. Meanwhile, three drops of fresh blood fell onto her hand, one after the other. Filled with terror she rushed home and asked for her child. Her husband brought her inside and confessed what he had done. He was about to show her the money that would free them from poverty, but it had turned into leaves. Then the father became mad and died from sorrow, but the mother went out and sought her child. She found it hanging from the tree and, with hot tears, took it down and carried it to the church at Rinn. It is lying there to this day, and the people look on it as a holy child. They also brought the Jews' Stone there. According to legend a shepherd cut down the birch tree, from which the child had hung, but when he attempted to carry it home he broke his leg and died from the injury.

Researcher Herta Herzog interviewed eighty Austrians and reported that reference to the "otherness" of the Jews is spontaneous. Jews are different, but unlike foreigners (Auslaender), the Jews have "always been here"; they have been here "for centuries," "for generations." In a few cases, it was pointed out that "the Jews have had a major share in shaping the Viennese culture." Less-educated respondents referred to Jewish department stores where they liked to shop, Jewish doctors, Jewish summer guests, Jewish friends of the parents, Jewish neighbors. "We lived with the Jews," one older lady said. The Jews are *anders als wir,* (different from us) e.g. in appearance, the Jewish way of life, customs, special skills. re: Jewish religious observance. A young secretary reports:

"Jews are different because of their religion. You see this already in their eating habits. You hear that they are very religious, more conscious of tradition than we are." This difference is discussed resentfully: "Jews are peculiar people. They live according to strict rules. Their way of thinking is different. Most people do not accept that. They feel people living in our country should adopt our customs." Jews are others and they also want to remain others. "They are not interested in us non-Jews," one representative respondent said. Jews consider themselves the "chosen people," therefore considering themselves superior and act condescendingly toward non-Jews.

In a few cases, the alleged non-accepting attitude of the Jews is not only taken from public discourse, but backed up by personal observation. The young secretary quoted before has this to add:

Jews want to have as little intercourse with non-Jews as possible. I know a Jewish girl who gets along with non-Jews but she does not respect them. I believe she is just envious because we can do what they are not permitted to do. I think the Jews judge us to be without morals or manners. The image of the Jews reflected in grassroots discourse is ambiguous. Public opinion, especially that conveyed by the younger generation born after the Holocaust, blames the Jews for feeling superior, resents their alleged tendency to keep apart, and their unwillingness to mix. They, too, see the otherness as difference, observed with a certain uneasy resentment unless one can find rationalizations to deny the superiority can be found.

Australia / New Zealand

According to genocide scholar Paul Bartop (1987) antisemitic cartoons and stereotypes in the populist "Bulletin" and in "Smith's Weekly" show the distinction between "good/bad Jews." British-style Australian Jews were good. Those Jews with foreign sounding accents and dress were deemed "bad Jews." Authorities rejected Polish Jewish immigrants during the 1920s as backward undesirables, and Jewish refugees from the Nazis because of their "non-assimilability." Many Australians thought the Jews had provoked persecution by the Nazis because they were parasitic, clannish, or unpatriotic though Australia's assimilated Jews had attained positions of status and power.

China / Japan

In China, the term for Jew is Youtai. This term equates to money, deviousness and meanness poverty, trustworthiness and warm-heartedness. Kaifeng may have been home to one of the first groups of immigrant Jews. Escaping the Eleventh Century crusades some Turkey Jews left for Kaifeng China. They built a synagogue in 1163 and may have numbered as many as 5,000 maintaining their cultural and religious identity into the Nineteenth Century.

Kohno Tetsu (1987) Japanese suggests that Japanese antisemitic folklore may have begun with the importing of the 19th Century version of Shakespeare's "Merchant of Venice." A second wave of folklore continued with the Protocols of the Elders of Zion was distributed during W.W I. By 1933, as Japan fell under military domination and fascist and Nazi influence grew, antisemitic propaganda flourished.

As is now known, some refugees were interned, but Japanese officials and diplomats saved others. Sympathy for the Jews, increased after the war and lessened after 1967. Jews were subject to moderate antisemitism, the peak periods of antisemitic hate did not occur until 1987 when Christian minister Uno Matsumi published a series of antisemitic tales of business savvy and secret rules for success. These tales caught the Japanese imagination and produced antisemitic outbreaks during the early 1990s. Here are some of the expressions that caught on at the time.

> *When a Jew sneezes at home every bank in the world will catch a cold.*
> *When three Jews are together they can deal with the global currency market.*

Christendom

Historian Michael Parenti and others have observed that the deicide slander began in the fourth gospel (falsely ascribed to the apostle John), where "the Jews" plotted against Jesus (earlier gospels referred more precisely to Pharisees, scribes, elders, and priests. By 20 CE an early church father named Origen charged that Jews had murdered Christ, for which they were to suffer. Later a leading church father, St. John Chrysostom informed his congregants that "God always hated the Jews. It is incumbent upon all Christians to hate the Jews." Parenti notes that papal proclamations, church sermons, pastoral letters, and council edicts all served to reinforce the myth (e.g. by 400 CE St. Augustine declared that the fate of the Jews is to be downtrodden and dispersed; they "forever will bear the guilt for the death of Jesus."). St. Thomas Aquinas considered it lawful and desirable "according to custom, to hold Jews, because of their crime in perpetual servitude." During the Protestant Reformation, when the Jews failed to flock to Martin Luther's version of Christianity, he lashed out. (Parenti, 2004 p.22)

Luther's invective against Jews took the form of *On Jews and their Lies* (1543) and other antisemitic tracts which recommended "First to set fire to their synagogues and houses be razed, their books be taken from them and rabbis forbidden to teach, safe conduct on highways be abolished. "Sixth I advise that usury be prohibited to them."

Know Christian, that next to the devil, thou has no enemy more cruel more venomous and violent than a true Jew.
        —Martin Luther

The Wandering Jew/Ahasuerus/Errant/Eternal Jew (see Lost Jew)

The Christian scribe Roger of Wendover (d. 1236) of the Monastery of St. Albans may have penned the first tale of the wandering Jew as a reaction immigration in England. (The uncle of Jesus was said to have taken a young Jesus to the British Isles and was still alive. The archbishop claimed to have seen St Joseph in Armenia renamed Cartaphilus). But it was not until the distribution of a chapbook from Leyden in 1602 that the myth gained popularity. The myth is as follows:

> A pilgrim from Armenia visited the monastery of St. Albans in 1228. He told of Cartapilus, the Jew who pushed and mocked Jesus on his was to the Crucifixion. Because of his mockery, he was condemned to live until the Second Coming. Cartapilus was later baptized as Joseph and living in Armenia. The parallels to Cain—his condemnation to eternal wandering was the punishment afforded to all Jews.

Heine places the tale in context.

> In a remote, peaceful valley a mother tells her children the gruesome tale. The little ones gather anxiously around the hearth. It is night. The post horn sounds outside: schacherjuden (Jewish crooks) drive past on their way to the Liepzig fair. We don't realize that we are the protagonists of this grisly tale. The white beard, its edge blackened once more by the passage of time—no barber can shave it off. The theme is that the Jew becomes doomed to a Sisyphusian restlessness retributive justice for the deicide. A Jew refuses to give

water in some versions, in other versions, hit Jesus on the back and Jesus retaliated with a the curse "I go but you will tarry until I return."—the shopkeeper fate is to wander the earth desperate to die but cannot.

In some versions the Jew is baptized and renamed Joseph, he grows to age 100 but then becomes thirty and his wandering continues. In other versions he is a shoemaker, a socialist, including a Salt Lake Utah Mormon Adventist version in 1868. There are multiple sightings as well. In Eastern European culture, it is considered 'good luck' to see the Wandering Jew. (see Lost Jew) [9]

Host Desecration

The tale upon which the Host myth was based, begins with the Tale of the Jewish Boy

The Tale of the Jewish Boy

> In Constantinople, a Jewish glazier son went to school with Christian boys. Once the son accompanied his school mates and partook of the 'Lords body and blood.' The child returned home and told his father. The Jewish father declared that he would avenge this offense to the law of Moses and threw the son into the oven. The boy's mother rushed to his rescue but seeing the heat of the fire she despaired and began wailing and shouting so that the city filled with her cries. When Christians inquired and were told of her calamity, they approached the fire only to see it subside and find the Jewish boy in it unscathed. The Jewish boy then converted with his mother and his example led many other Jews to do so while his father was thrown into the oven.

Antisemitism expert Gavin Langmuir (1990) suggests that the Host desecration myth grew out of Christian insecurities surrounding the doctrine of transubstantiation, e.g. the body and blood of Christ is the consecrated sacramental bread and wine. Christian theologians grappled with some of the obvious biological problems which attended this belief, such as the implications of excrement. Historian Miri Rubin documents that the first Host desecration allegation occurred in Paris 1290.

> The tale begins as a poor Christian woman is tempted by a Jew to whom she owed money. The debt would be canceled if she would merely bring him from Easter communion the Host. She may have simply keep the Host in her mouth and remove it secretly. Once he had the Host, the Jew subject to tests to see if it was transubstantiated as the body of Christ. He wanted to see "whether the insane things which Christians prattle about are true." He stabbed at it with his knife, but it remained uncut. Even so, it began to bleed. He tortured it in various ways, nailing it to a board, throwing it into a fire, and boiling it. The Host remained whole and bleeding, until the boiling, when it turned into a crucifix above the pot. The Jew was amazed, but was still unconvinced. (Seeing such a spectacle immediately converted his wife and children)

There are several versions of Host Desecration.

> Version A. The Jews assemble for Passover with a host they obtained from a greedy sacristan; after they pierce it blood flows, and they toss the host onto a dung pile (Dungerhaufen) next to the house, where pigs are rummaging. The pigs raise a miraculous hue and cry, the burghers come to the scene, and the malefactors are discovered. All the Jews of Pulkau are seized and burned alive on a pyre at a place called the Judengrube, and the houses of the Jews are torn down by order of Duke Albrecht II. In the place of the rabbi's house, where the crime took place, a chapel is built.

> Version B. With the help of a sacristan from Retz, local Jews obtain a consecrated host, which they pierce with sharp knives as an expression of their anti-Christian hatred; blood flows from the host and a luminous apparition of the Christ Child appears over the criminals. Confused and hoping to conceal their crime, the Jews cast the host into a domestic well (Hausbrunnen); the inhabitants see the water turn blood red and the host swimming around in the water. The Jews try to dispose of the host again by feeding it to a pig; instead of eating it, the beast kneels piously before the host and begins to scream, alerting the faithful. Priests elevate the holy host and carry it in procession to the parish church of St. Michael. Finally, the Jews are condemned to death by fire;

the houses of the Jews are torn down by order of Duke Albrecht II, and a chapel is built on the site of the rabbi's house (and the well incorporated into the new sanctuary).

Version C presumably follows the basic desecration and miracle motifs common to A and B, especially the piercing with knives and the Christ Child apparition, but deviates on the matter of concealment and discovery: the Jews deposit the host in a woodland spring (or quarry?) outside of town. (According to what may be a later addition, the host swims back into town via the Pulkau River and reappears inside the domestic well, where it emits miraculous signals, alerting the townspeople to its presence.) (Merback, 2005)

To bolster with the antisemitic legend, various church leaders have at times become creative. In Koreneuburg, Austria, a cleric sprinkled some blood on an unconsecrated Host and displayed it in the local church. He later confessed to the bishop of Passau. It was revered by the faithful as a true host until it was completely destroyed by insects and moths. When a second cleric spattered blood on another unconsecrated Host and admitted to it the second host was still revered. During some celebrations Jews were ordered to remain in their homes when the Host was processed through the streets re: protecting the Host from ridicule, sorcery, and the evil eye.

The implications for Host Descration were quite different than that of the Wandering Jew myth. Throughout the Middle Ages, the charge of Host Desecration may have killed from at least 10,000 Jews with some estimates tenfold that number. Perhaps forty Jewish villages were razed throughout Germany in the little known Rindfleisch and Armleder massacres of 1298 and 1336.

Blood Libel/Ritual Murder

As deadly as the Host Descration myths have been, the most enduring anti-semitic myth is that of the blood libel. Beginning with Greek scholar Apion (First century C.E.) the origins of the ritual murder accusation have stood the test of time and space. It was Apion who initially accused the Jews of preparing a human sacrifice for the Temple. Other Christian documents suggest early support for the myth as well e.g. *Socrates Scholastics and The Jews commit Another Outrage upon the Christians and are Punished.* Over the years ritual murder libels continued with hundreds of Jews tried and sentenced to death. For instance, flagellating roving bands of Christians in 1349 accused the Jews of Chillon, Switzerland of plotting to kill Christians via poisoning wells, wine and food destroying approximately 300 Jewish communities.

Chaucer's *Canterbury Tales* includes a variation of the blood libel called *The Prioress's Tale.* (For related antisemitic tales see Langland's Piers Plowman and Croxton Play of the Sacrament). The Prioress begins with a recommendation. To attain the tale's purity, the prioress (nun) states that she must recite the tale in the voice of a twelve-year-old.

The tale begins with an innocent Christian child walks through the Jewish ghetto on his way to school, singing Alma Redemptoris Mater ("O gracious mother of the redeemer"). The Jews, outraged, hire a killer who seizes the child, cuts his throat, and throws the body in a privy/toilet. The child's distraught mother searches for him throughout the ghetto. Wondrously the child continues to sing. The provost (judge) comes, puts the Jews to death, and has the child carried to the church where the abbot sprinkles him with holy water and he explains. There the child explains that the Virgin Mary laid a grain upon his tongue and he will sing until it is removed. When the grain is removed the child gives up the ghost and is buried as a martyr.

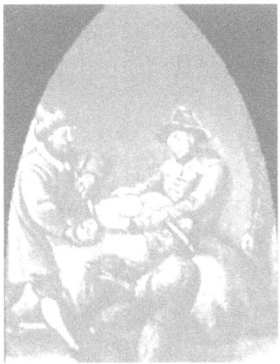

At times, sainthoods have been revoked e.g. St. Simon and St. Hugh after investigations revealed that 'the Jews' did not kill local children. The following are a list of others who were not investigated.

Andrel von Rinn (b. 1459; d. 1462)
Anderl, a three year-old boy who became the focus of a blood-libel cult in the Seventeenth Century. In several illustrations, Anderl is a child being held down and having his throat slit and his blood collected in a bowl or bucket. The killers are clearly marked as Jews by their clothes and turbans (one form of the "special mark" Jews were forced to carry by Church decree). On some depictions the text reads: "Sie schneiden dem Marterer, die Gurgl ab und nemen alles Blut von Ihm", literally they cut throat of the martyr and take/drain all blood from him. The myth of the blood libel was that the blood of a Christian child was used

to make Passover matzohs and as Brown University historian David I. Kertzer has noted was referenced by a Church newspaper up through the 20th Century. A cultus of Anderl von Rinn began in 1621 and by the late 17th century Anderl was established throughout the Tyrol, together with other boys who had supposedly been killed by Jews (e.g. Simon of Trent). The body of Anderl was transferred from the church to the churchyard of Judenstein in 1985 and in 1994 the cult was officially forbidden. Some people make a procession to his grave every year. [Feast Day July 12].

—Conrad of Weissensee, d. 1303

—Dominic of Val/Dominguito d 1250 A 7-yr-old altar boy at the Cathedral of Saragossa was kidnapped by Jews and nailed against a wall. His feast is celebrated throughout Aragon." [Feast Day August 31]

—Herbert of Huntingdon, d. 1180

—Hugh of Lincoln (1247–August, 1255)
The boy disappeared on July 31, and his body was discovered in a well on August 29. Shortly after his disappearance, a local Jew named Copin (or Jopin) admitted to killing the child after he was threatened with torture. In his confession Copin stated that it was the custom of the Jews to crucify a Christian child every year. Copin was executed, and the story would have ended were it not for a series of events that coincided with the disappearance. Some six months earlier, King Henry III had sold his rights to tax the Jews to his brother, Richard, Earl of Cornwall. Having lost this source of income, he decided that he was eligible for the Jews' money if they were convicted of crimes. As a result, some ninety Jews were arrested and held in the Tower of London, while they were charged with involvement in the ritual murder. Eighteen of them were hanged—it was the first time ever that the civil government handed out a death sentence for ritual murder—and King Henry was able to take over their property. The remainder were fined, pardoned and set free, most likely because Richard, who saw a potential threat to his own source of income, intervened on their behalf with his brother. The Cathedral in Lincoln was beginning to benefit from the episode, since Hugh was seen as a Christian martyr, and sites associated with his life became objects of pilgrimage. The legend surrounding Hugh that emerged received the backing of popular culture, and his story became the subject of poetry and folksongs. Tourists devoted to Hugh of Lincoln flocked to the city as late as the early 20th cen-

tury, when a well was constructed in the former Jewish neighborhood of Jews' Court and advertised as the well in which Hugh's body was found. In 1955, the Anglican Church replaced the shrine at Lincoln Cathedral with an apologia. A Feast day: July 27 was established.

—Joanniken von Siegburg, d. 1287

—Lorenzino Sossio, d. 1485 age 5, killed on Good Friday. [Feast Day.April 15]

—Louis or Ludwig of Ravensburg d. 1429 Murdered at Easter. [Feast Day April 30].

—Nino of La Guardia d.1491
In 1490, a New Christian named Benito García who worked as a wool comber was traveling from town to town selling his wares (one source says that he was returning from a pilgrimage.) He stopped at an inn where a party of drunken men broke into his knapsack. While going through his goods, they found a wafer, like those consecrated ones used in communion. Laymen could not legally be in possession of these wafers and the thieves realized this was a major crime. Turning García in to the authorities would bring a bigger prize than that which they could obtain from selling his stolen possessions. They turned García over to the law.

The magistrate who heard the case was Dr. Pedro de Villada who had worked closely with the Inquisition in the past and had hopes of being elevated to a judgeship in the Inquisition. De Villada insisted that García admit to judaising and that he had stolen the consecrated host for use in a conjuration in which the host and a human heart would be used to cast a spell causing all Christians to die raving mad so the Jews would obtain their wealth.

García refused to admit guilt and he was subjected to two hundred lashes followed by the dreaded water torture and the "garrote," sharp cords twisted tightly around arms and legs. He finally broke down and admitted he had been a good Christian for thirty years but that for the last five years he practiced Judaism whenever he found it safe to do so. This was not enough for Pedro de Villada, García must name his co-conspirators. García implicated Juan de Ocaña, the brothers Mosé and Yucé Franco and their father Ça Franco, and several others, a total of six conversos and five Jews, including three who were deceased. All who were still alive were arrested and tortured. Yucé Franco fell ill in prison and, fearing that he was near death, he asked for a physician and a rabbi. A physician was sent, but the "rabbi" was actually a priest in disguise. Yucé, in his delirium, told the priest/rabbi that he and his friends were accused of planning the ritual murder of a Christian child.

—Pedro de Arbués died 1484

Pedro de Arbues died in the Saragossa Cathedral at age 43 at the hand of The Jews. Arbués was canonized(sainthood) by Pope Pius IX in 1867. The Catholic Encyclopedia notes that Peter performed the duties with zeal and justice. Although the enemies of the Inquisition accuse him of cruelty, it is certain that not a single sentence of death can be traced to him … The Marranos, however, whom he had punished hated and resolved to do away with him. One night while kneeling in prayer before the altar of Our Lady in the metropolitan church, where he used to recite the office with his brother canons, they attacked him, and hired assassins inflicted several wounds from which he died two days after.

—Richard of Pontoise/Paris, d. 1179

—Robert of Bury St. Edmunds d. 1181

Martyred by The Jews on Good Friday and is entombed in the church at Edmundsbury.

—Rudolf of Berne, d. 1294

Simon of Trent

One of the more embarrasing sainthoods is that of Simon of Trent, Patron Saint of Antisemitism. Born in Trento, Italy, (d.1475), Simon's (Unverdorben) disappearance was linked to the town's Jews after several admitted to the deed. (The confessions were extracted under torture. Po-Chia's (1992) analysis demonstrates how Jews could be made, not only to confess, but to provide the required detail and evidence which was expected of them). The tale is as follows:

> An itinerant Franciscan preacher (Bernardo da Feltre) delivered series of sermons vilifying the Trent Jewish community. When Simon went missing (Easter 1475) his father concluded that the child was kidnapped and murdered by The Jews. According to the father's statements, The Jews used Simon's blood to make matza for their Passover meal.

Leaders of the Jewish community were arrested, and seventeen of them confessed under torture. Fifteen of them, including Samuel, the head of the community, were sentenced to death and burned at the stake. The local Catholic Church venerated Simon with over one hundred miracles directly attributed to "Little Saint Simon." Within a year of his disappearance, his cult spread across Italy and Germany. The cultus/beatification occurred in 1588 by Pope Sixtus V. In 1965, the Church began to investigate the story of Saint Simon and opened the trial records declaring the episode a fraud. Pope Paul VI invalidated the beatification of Saint Simon and the shrine erected to him was dismantled. In 2001 the local authorities of the Autonomous Province of Trento promoted a common Catholic and Jewish prayer at the site.

Hundreds of ritual murders by Jews were thought to have occurred. Among the more famous false accusations is that of The Jews in Damascus (1840) who were accused of ritually murdering clergy—Father Tommaso. The accusation resulted in seventy Jews being tortured. The witch-hunt concluded when the local sultan (Abdul Mejid) spoke out against it. In other cases, Catholic papal bulls had been issued (1247, 1259, 1272, 1422, 1540, 1759) though the Vatican periodical *Civilta Cattolica* continued to offer "documented proof" of the legend from 1881–1914. Other blood libel cases include Tisza-Eslar Hungary (1882) Polna Czech Republic (1899) and as far away as Lima Peru when in 1639, more than 80 Jewish conversos were killed in an auto-da-fe.

Variations of the blood libel charge may included the trials of Russia's Beilis and the U.S.'s Leo Frank in 1913. Edgar Morin reminds us that a "Rumour in Orleans" of Jews kidnapping girls in Orleans France 1969 produced violent vigilante action against Jewish shopowners.

—Werner or Oberwesel, d. 1287.
Employed by Jews who were accused of murdering the fourteen year old on Holy Thursday, just after he had received Communion. The "good Werner" was found floating in the Rhein river and his corpse had a halo which healed and sufficient proof of the Jews involvement. Jews were persecuted in Oberwesel and neighboring villages between 1286 and 1289 at times halted by the emperor's intervention. According to historians Perry and Schweitzer (2002), as late as 1889, books graphically depicted how 'the Jews' hung Werner up by the legs and opened his veins to drain his blood. [Feast Day. April 19]

—William of Norwich (See England)

—Vierge de Valreas (France) d. 1247
Two year old girl found dead during Passion Week. The Jews of Valreas were accused, property seized, jailed, tortured (breasts cut off women, penis cut-off men) into confessing the murder

Czech Republic

The nature and extent of antisemitic myths may be determined by examining literary works e.g. Mácha's Cikáni (The Gypsies, 1835), where Lea, a Jewish girl is struck by a gypsy's lament that "my nation is scattered," and sings her own moving song on this motif. The Jews are portrayed as sympathetic to other's suffering, but it is still one-dimensional, and Jews still fit the stereotype.

Rural fiction of 19th Century Czech prose generally embraced antisemitic stereotypes. Jews were depicted as wandering junk dealers who arrive in a town and gradually get rich by preying on the peasants—lending to them at high interest rates, ruining them with alcohol, and eventually repossessing their land.

Being Czech and being Jewish were considered separate domains in the Czech mind. Czech writers perceived Jews as agents of Germanization, supporting German-language schools and undermining local officials from the Czech national cause. Such portrayals were common to a whole range of writers, The poet and journalist Jan Neruda (1834–1891) wrote pamphlets such as "Prostrach židovský" (For Fear of the Jews, 1869), in which he calls for an "emancipation from the Jews." Neruda maligns them for their unchanging foreignness, for their inferiorities intellectually, spiritually and physiologically. Other depictions e.g. Kolar's play Pražský žid (The Prague Jew; 1871), were more positive but still stereotypical e.g. The rich Jew Eliab donates money to the defeated Czech cause and refuses to flee his homeland. There is also Vrchlický (1853–1912) epic poem Bar Kochba (1897), with parallels between the Jewish nation and the Czechs, both seeking to preserve their own identity in a foreign empire.

http://64.233.167.104/search?q=cache:3rvmBECWfhoJ:yivo.org/pdf/czech_lit.pdf+antisemitic+tales+czech&hl=en&ct=cln

England

The most famous of all blood libels was William of Norwich which appears to have triggered the above wave of European Christian libels.

William of Norwich (see Blood Libel)

According to the boy's own family, he was enticed away on Monday, March 21, 1144, to become a scullion of the Archdeacon of Norwich, and was not heard of again till Saturday, March 26, when his uncle, cousin, and brother found his body, covered with sand, in Thorpe Wood, near Norwich, with the head shaven and with marks of puncture by thorns. Although there were signs of life in the body, it was reburied in the same place; and Godwin Sturt, the boy's uncle, at the next synod, accused the Jews of having murdered William, whereupon the prior of Lewis Priory claimed the body as that of a martyr, and the canons of Norwich Cathedral seized it for themselves. The boy's brother Robert and his uncle Godwin were appointed officials in the monastery on the strength of their relationship to the martyr; and his mother was buried in the graveyard of the monastery, somewhat to the scandal of the monks. No action was taken against the accused Jews, though it was asserted that the boy William had been seen entering the house of a Jew named Deusaie or Eleazar, and a report was brought from Theobald, a converted Jew of Cambridge, that it was the custom of Jews to sacrifice a boy at Passover at some place chosen by lot, and that the lot for that year had fallen on Norwich. The royal sheriff, in whose jurisdiction the Jews were, refused to take notice of the accusation, although he was himself indebted to the Jews, and would have been benefited personally if they had been proved guilty.

It has been suggested that the boy's relatives in a fit of religious exaltation attempted to gain increased sanctity for themselves and for the lad by making him undergo the form of crucifixion on Good Friday, March 25. During the process, the boy had fell into a fit, which alarmed his relatives, who thereupon buried him in Thorpe Wood, near their residence. To divert suspicion, they accused the Jews, although the process of crucifixion would be quite unfamiliar to them, and obtained some sort of confirmation from the convert Theobald. Later, the legend of the martyr was considerably developed by Thomas of Capgrade (d. 1494). It was claimed that the Jews were met as they were carrying the body in a bag to Thorpe Wood, on the opposite side from the Jewry outside the city, which they would have had to traverse. The person who encountered them kept silent, it was alleged, at the order of the sheriff, who had been bribed by the Jews. On his refusal to testify, a fierce light from heaven pointed out the place of martyrdom to a man, who found the lad's body disfigured with stigmata and hanging from a tree. Nothing of all this is found in the earliest form of the legend as related by Thomas of Monmouth, although the supernatural light appeared in German. [Feast day: March 26].

The Jew of Tewkesbury (see Imprisoned Jew at Magdeburg)

A Jew falls into a public cesspit on a Saturday and refuses to extract himself out of reverence for Jewish law, making excretion cognate with the Jewish Sabbath.

Historian Anthony Bale (2003) takes medieval historians to task for manufacturing whole stereotypes of English Jewry as did Chronica Majora of Matthew Paris of Hertfordshire (1200–1259) Of the Jewish financier Abraham of Berkhamsted, he wrote:

> There was a certain quite rich Jew, Abraham by name but not in faith, who lived and had property in Berkhamsted and Wallingford. He was friendly with Earl Richard [of Cornwall] for some improper reason or other. He had a beautiful and faithful wife called Floria. In order to dishonor Christ the more, this Jew bought a nicely carved and painted statue of the blessed Virgin, as usual nursing her son at her bosom. This image the Jew set up in his latrine and, what is thoroughly dishonorable and ignominious to mention, as it were in blasphemy of the Blessed Virgin, he inflicted a most filthy and unmentionable thing on it, daily and nightly, and ordered his wife to do the same. Noticing this after some days, by reason of her sex, she felt sorry and, going there secretly washed the dirt from the face of the disgracefully defiled statue. When the Jew her husband found out the truth of this, he impiously and secretly suffocated his wife. However, these crimes were discovered and the Jew, clearly proved guilty, although there were other grounds for putting him to death, was thrust into the foulest dungeon in the Tower of London. In a bid to be freed, he promised most positively that he would prove all the Jews in England to be the basest traitors. Thereupon he was basely accused by almost all the English Jews, who tried to put him to death, but Earl Richard spoke up for him. So the Jews, accusing him of clipping coins and other serious crimes, offered the earl a thousand marks to stop protecting him, which however the earl refused because the Jew was said to be his. This Jew Abraham then paid the king seven hundred marks so that, with the help of the earl, he could be freed from the life imprisonment to which he had been condemned.

Ethiopia

During the weeks surrounding Selassie's outster and Col. Mariam's coup, an estimated 2,500 Jews were killed and 7,000 became homeless. After taking office in 1977, Israeli Prime Minister Menachem Begin was eager to facilitate the rescue of Ethiopia's Jews. Israel entered into a period of selling arms to the Mariam government in exchange that Ethiopia would allow Jews to leave for Israel. By 1977,

Begin asked President Mengistu to allow 200 Ethiopian Jews to leave for Israel aboard an Israeli military jet that had emptied its military cargo and was returning to Israel. Mariam agreed, in what was the precursor to Operation Moses. In the early 1980's, Ethiopia forbade the practice of Judaism and the teaching of Hebrew (previously Jews were not permitted to own land). Numerous members of the Beta Israel were imprisoned on fabricated charges of being "Zionist spies," and Jewish religious leaders, Kesim, (sing. Kes) were harassed and monitored by the government. The Beta Israel's position became precarious as time progressed. Over 8,000 Beta Israel went to Israel between 1977 and 1984 followed by 1984's Operation Moses.

Ethiopia's Beta Israel (falasha) Jews have been victims of long standing myths that parallel many mainstream Christian fantasies regarding Jews. They include: religious disputes, blood, purity, slavery, conversion, and supernatural powers that mark them as Buda (hyena people) and keep them most vulnerable to violence and antisemitic attacks. As Buda, Jews there are thought to magically transform themselves into hyenas at night and steal from their Christian neighbors. (Salamon 1999) [10]

France

In a sociological analysis of French newspapers, pamphlets, and books published in 1889, Marc Angenot (1984) examined widespread antisemitic texts, jokes, and caricatures and concludes that antisemitism was an omnipresent component of social discourse and detected in all political and ideological trends. An analysis by Matard-Bonucci (2005) similarly observed the pervasiveness of antisemitic folklore in Nineteenth Century France that acts to fuel the current antisemitic myths.

Unique to France and Germany was the myth of a secret world conspiracy originating in tthe 18th Century regarding the Freemasons. Exactly how the stonecutters became aligned with the folkloric Jew remains uncertain linkages have been reported to the Illumanati, the secret organization which is thought to control all world affairs. In 1797, Abbé Augustin Barruél published *Memoirs Illustrating the History of Jacobinism* outlining a vivid conspiracy theory involving the Knights Templar, the Rosicrucians, the Jacobins and the Illuminati, during the course of which Barruél blamed all of what he regarded as the disasters of his times such as the French Revolution on the several groups pointing primaril to 'the Jews.' The Jewish Freemasonry conspiracy was thought to undermine all social order by creating new modern movements such as liberalism, socialism, capitalism.

Germany (Medieval)

German folklore has its origins alongside Scandinavia and England in Germanic mythology. It reflects a similar mix of influences: a pre-Christian/Norse mythology; magical characters (sometimes recognizably pre-Christian) and various regional 'character' stories. As in Scandinavia, when belief in the old gods disappeared, remnants persisted e.g. Holda, a "supernatural" patron of spinning; the Lorelei, a dangerous Rhine siren; the fairy Berchta; the Weisse Frau, a water fairy said to protect children; the Wild Hunt; the giant Rübezahl; changeling legends; and the elf, dwarf, kobold and erlking. Other folklore includes Knecht Ruprecht, a Santa Claus like character; the Yule witch Lutzelfrau, the Osterhase (Easter Bunny); and Walpurgisnacht, a spring festival derived from pagan customs. The tales include the famous Pied Piper of Hamelin, and the lesser known trickster hero Till Eulenspiegel, the Town Musicians of Bremen and Faust. Philosopher and nationalist Johann Gottfried von Herder (1744–1803) was said to have inspired the Brothers Grimm, Goethe and others. For instance, folklore elements, such as the Rhine Maidens and the Grimms' *The Tale of a Boy Who Went Forth to Learn Fear,* formed part of the source material for Richard Wagner's opera cycle *Der Ring des Nibelungen.*

The Bloody Children of the Jews

> Between about 1492 and 1500 in many areas of Germany, for example in Brandenburg and in Mecklenburg, the Jews were committing all kinds of godless sins, especially the desecration of the holy sacrament. For this reason they were expelled from the country by their lords. Duke Bogislav of Pomerania was among those who expelled the Jews, many of whom at that time were living at Damm near Stettin, at Bart, and in all the small towns in the country. Among these Jews there were a man and a woman who had themselves baptized. The Duke allowed them to stay, and they moved to the vicinity of Lake Trieb. However, their baptism was only for the sake of appearance, and in reality they remained Jews. For this reason, they were visibly punished by God. Every time the woman gave birth to a child, it came to the earth with a bloody hand. Because the Christian women observed this, everyone shied away from them, and no one wanted to have anything to do with them. Therefore the Jew and his wife moved away from Lake Trieb, first to Lassahn, and then to Usedom. But the curse followed them wherever they went, until they finally underwent a spiritual conversion and confessed that previously they had remained Jews in their hearts.

The Cholera Children

> Three Jews carry gold, silver and precious stones which they hope to sell at a profit. On the way they come across a horseman. "Don't ride so fast sir." they call to the horseman. "Let three poor Jews come with you for we fear for our lives on the road!" The young man took pity on the Jews. (The horseman, an orphan because of cholera, was brought up by a merchant taken into the service of a sultan and offers them his protection). He saves them from robbers and in the end even rescues them from the gallows when they are wrongly condemned to death. But then he leaves them because they will not listen to his advice and by ignoring it, always ends up in trouble. Jews are obstinate.

The Jewish Pig/Der Judensau

The Jew as pig or Jew's sow (judensau) was a common subject of Christian religious art. It depicted bearded rabbis sucking the excrement from a huge pig. The scene is overseen approvingly by Satan. Displays of the Judensau are in front of some of the great cathedrals of Europe as well as a municipal display on the main bridge into Frankfurt. The tale is as follows:

> A rabbi was arguing with his friends whether or not Christ was the Messiah and met Jesus. If you are truly the Messiah then you can surely see what lies beneath this barrel next to me" the skeptical rabbi said. (the rabbi thought some pigs were napping there but the pigs had been replaced by his own son).

When Jesus told him that it was his son, the rabbi sneered so Christ turned the son into a pig and walked away.

Jew in the Bush (Grimms)

Once upon a time there was a rich man who had a servant who served him diligently and honestly. Every morning he was the first one out of bed, and at night the last one to go to bed. Whenever there was a difficult job that nobody wanted to do, he was always the first to volunteer. He never complained at any of this, but was contented with everything and always happy.

When his year was over, his master gave him no wages, thinking, "That is the smartest thing to do, for it will save me something. He won't leave me, but will gladly stay here working for me."

The servant said nothing, but did his work the second year as he had done before, and when at the end of this year he again received no wages, he still stayed on without complaining. When the third year had passed, the master thought it over, then put his hand into his pocket, but pulled out nothing. However, this time the servant said, "Master, I have served you honestly for three years. Be so good as to give me what by rights I have coming to me. I would like to be on my way and see something else of the world." "Yes, my good servant," answered the old miser, "you have served me without complaint, and you shall be kindly rewarded."

With this he put his hand into his pocket, then counted out three hellers one at a time, saying, "There, you have a heller for each year. That is a large and generous reward. Only a few masters would pay you this much."

The good servant, who understood little about money, put his wealth into his pocket, and thought, "Ah, now that I have a full purse, why should I worry and continue to plague myself with hard work?"

So he set forth, uphill and down, singing and jumping for joy. Now it came to pass that as he was passing by a thicket a little dwarf stepped out, and called to him, "Where are you headed, Brother Merry? You don't seem to be burdened down with cares."

"Why should I be sad?" answered the servant. "I have everything I need. Three years' wages are jingling in my pocket.

"How much is your treasure?" the dwarf asked him.

"How much? Three hellers in real money, precisely counted."

"Listen," said the dwarf, "I am a poor and needy man. Give me your three hellers. I can no longer work, but you are young and can easily earn your bread."

Now because the servant had a good heart and felt pity for the dwarf, he gave him his three hellers, saying, "In God's name, I won't miss them."

Then the dwarf said, "Because I see that you have a good heart I will grant you three wishes, one for each heller. They shall all be fulfilled."

"Aha," said the servant. "You are a miracle worker. Well, then, if it is to be so, first of all I wish for a blowpipe that will hit everything I aim at; second, for a fiddle, that when I play it, anyone who hears it will have to dance; and third, that whenever I ask a favor of anyone, it will be granted."

"You shall have all that," said the dwarf. He reached into the bush, and what do you think, there lay a fiddle and a blowpipe, all ready, just as if they had been ordered. He gave them to the servant, saying, "No one will ever be able to deny any request that you might make."

"What more could my heart desire?" said the servant to himself, and went merrily on his way.

Soon afterward he met a Jew with a long goatee, who was standing listening to a bird singing high up in the top of a tree.

"One of God's own miracles," he shouted, "that such a small creature should have such a fearfully loud voice. If only it were mine! If only someone would sprinkle some salt on its tail!"

"If that is all you want," said the servant, "then the bird shall soon be down here." He took aim, hit it precisely, and the bird fell down into a thorn hedge.

"Rogue," he said to the Jew, "Go and fetch the bird out for yourself."

"My goodness," said the Jew, "don't call me a rogue, sir, but I will be the dog and get the bird out for myself. After all, you're the one who shot it."

Then he lay down on the ground and began crawling into the thicket. When he was in the middle of the thorns, the good servant could not resist the temptation to pick up his fiddle and begin to play.

The Jew's legs immediately began to move, and he jumped up. The more the servant fiddled the better went the dance. However, the thorns ripped apart the Jew's shabby coat, combed his beard, and pricked and pinched him all over his body.

"My goodness," cried the Jew, "what do I want with your fiddling? Stop playing, sir. I don't want to dance."

But the servant did not listen to him, and thought, "You have fleeced people often enough, and now the thorn hedge shall do the same to you." He began to play all over again, so that the Jew had to jump even higher, leaving scraps from his coat hanging on the thorns.

"Oh, woe is me!" cried the Jew. "I will give the gentleman anything he asks, if only he quits fiddling, even a purse filled with gold."

"If you are so generous," said the servant, "then I will stop my music. But I must praise the singular way that you dance to it." Then he took his purse he went on his way.

The Jew stood there quietly watching the servant until he was far off and out of sight, and then he screamed out with all his might, "You miserable musician, you beer-house fiddler! Wait until I catch you alone. I will chase you until you wear the soles off your shoes. You ragamuffin, just put a groschen in your mouth, so that you will be worth six hellers." He continued to curse as fast as he could speak. As soon as he had thus refreshed himself a little, and caught his breath again, he ran into the town to the judge.

"Judge, sir," he said, "Oh, woe is me! See how a godless man has robbed me and abused me on the open road. A stone on the ground would feel sorry for me. My clothes are ripped into shreds. My body is pricked and scratched to pieces. And what little I owned has been taken away with my purse—genuine ducats, each piece more beautiful than the others. For God's sake, let the man be thrown into prison."

The judge asked, "Was it a soldier who cut you up like that with his saber?"

"God forbid," said the Jew. "He didn't have a naked dagger, but rather a blowpipe hanging from his back, and a fiddle from his neck. The scoundrel can easily be recognized."

The judge sent his people out after him. They found the good servant, who had been walking along quite slowly. And they found the purse with the money on him as well.

When he was brought before the judge he said, "I did not touch the Jew, nor take his money. He offered it to me freely, so that I would stop fiddling, because he could not stand my music."

"God forbid!" cried the Jew. "He is reaching for lies like flies on the wall."

The judge did not believe his story, and said, "That is a poor excuse. No Jew would do that." And because he had committed robbery on the open road, the good servant was sentenced to the gallows.

As he was being led away, the Jew screamed after him, "You good-for-nothing. You dog of a musician. Now you will receive your well earned reward."

The servant walked quietly up the ladder with the hangman, but on the last rung he turned around and said to the judge, "Grant me just one request before I die."

"Yes," said the judge, "if you do not ask for your life."

"I do not ask for life," answered the servant, "but let me play my fiddle one last time."

The Jew cried out miserably, "For God's sake, do not allow it! Do not allow it!"

But the judge said, "Why should I not grant him this short pleasure? It has been promised to him, and he shall have it." In any event, he could not have refused because of the gift that had been bestowed on the servant.

The Jew cried, "Oh, woe is me! Tie me up. Tie me up tightly."

The good servant took his fiddle from his neck, and made ready. As he played the first stroke, they all began to quiver and shake: the judge, the clerks, and the court officials. The rope fell out of the hand of the one who was going to tie up the Jew.

At the second stroke they all lifted their legs. The hangman released the good servant and made ready to dance.

At the third stroke everyone jumped up and began to dance. The judge and the Jew were out in front and were the best at jumping. Soon everyone who had gathered in the marketplace out of curiosity was dancing with them, old and young, fat and thin, all together with each other. Even the dogs that had run along with the crowd stood up on their hind legs and hopped along as well. The longer he played, the higher the dancers jumped, until they were knocking their heads together and crying out terribly.

Finally the judge, quite out of breath, shouted, "I will give you your life, but just stop fiddling."

The good servant listened to this, then took his fiddle, hung it around his neck again, and climbed down the ladder. He went up to the Jew, who was lying upon the ground gasping for air, and said, "You rogue, now confess where you got the money, or I will take my fiddle off my neck and begin to play again."

"I stole it. I stole it," he cried. "But you have honestly earned it."

With that the judge had the Jew led to the gallows and hanged as a thief.

(For a critique of Jew in the Bush antisemtism see Ruth Bottigheimer's (1987) Grimm's bad girls and bold boys. New Haven: Yale University Press)

The Chapel of the Holy Body at Magdeburg (see Host Desecration)

In the year 1315 a thief broke into Saint Paul's Church in Magdeburg during the night and stole a box containing consecrated hosts, which were used for the sacrament. The next morning he took them to Saint Peter's Church, intending to place them on the altar there. However, he changed his mind and threw the sacrament into a puddle between the paving stones behind the churchyard. He turned the box over to the Jews. Now it happened that someone came by with a water cart that was used to carry water from the River Elbe for the purpose of beer brewing. The horses stopped when they came to the place where the sacrament was lying, and they would not proceed. The cart driver became aware of the sacrament lying there, and a miller, who just happened upon the scene, picked it up with his sword. They soon discovered who the thief was. He was captured in the clothing market with the Jews and was afterward dragged to death. In commemoration of this miracle, the citizens built a chapel where the sacrament had been found. The chapel was named the Chapel of the Holy Body. Inside they painted a mural depicting the event and hung the sword that had been used to pick up the sacrament. The chapel was still standing behind the Saint Mary Magdalene Convent until a short time ago. One could enter the chapel either from the convent or from the churchyard. Inside the chapel there was also a well and an iron bucket with which one could draw water.

The Expulsion of the Jews from Prussia

The Jews were expelled from Prussia under Grand Master Ludolph König, for the following reason: At the time of this Grand Master in the city of Schwetz there lived a fisherman who had but little luck fishing on the Weichsel River and who was therefore very poor. One day a Jew came to him and taught him how he could take a consecrated host, place it in his net, and thus catch as many fish as he wanted. The poor man followed the Jew's advice. Whenever he participated in the sacrament of the Lord's supper, he did not swallow the Lord's flesh but instead secretly took it from his mouth, then caught many fish with it, and became a rich man. One year afterward the Jew was imprisoned for other misdeeds, and he also confessed to what he had taught the fisherman. The fisherman learned what had happened, jumped quickly into his boat, and escaped. However, the Jew was executed, and all of his fellow Jews were expelled from the land. From that time forth no Jews have been allowed to enter Prussia, except to attend the Twelfth-Night Fair at Thorn, and even then they must be escorted and must wear a sign on their clothing so they can be recognized.

The Girl Who Was Killed by Jews (Grimms)

In the year 1267 in Pforzheim an old woman, driven by greed, sold an inno-cent seven-year-old girl to the Jews. The Jews gagged her to keep her from cry-ing out, cut open her veins, and surrounded her in order to catch her blood with cloths. The child soon died from the torture, and they weighted her down with stones and threw her into the Enz River. A few days later little Margaret reached her little hand above the streaming water. A number of peo-ple, including the Margrave himself soon assembled. Some boatmen suc-ceeded in pulling the child out of the water. She was still alive, but as soon as she had called for vengeance against her murderers, she died. Suspicion fell upon the Jews, and they were all summoned to appear. As they approached the corpse, blood began to stream from its open wounds. The Jews and the old woman confessed the evil deed and were executed. The child's coffin, with an inscription, stands next to the bell rope near the entrance to the palace church at Pforzheim. Children of the members the boatmen's guild unanimously pass the legend from generation to generation that at that time the Margrave rewarded their ancestors by freeing them from sentry duty in the city of Pforzheim "as long as the sun and the moon continue to shine." At the same time they were given the right to be represented by twenty-four boatmen, car-rying arms and musical instruments, who parade and stand watch over the city every year at the Carnival celebration. This privilege applies even to this day.

The Good Cloth (Grimms)

A Jewish trader buys a magic cloth from a girl. Anything wrapped in the cloth will turn to gold. He enters scene with a street cry such as could be heard in any town. "Fine new cloths fore sale or exchange against the old ones, come and see my wares!" Then the Jew turns into a dog the two girls become hens, the hens turn into people once more and batter the dog to death.

Judel, the Jew Ghost (Grimms)

If the Judel wont let the children sleep, give him soemthing to play with. When children laugh in their sleep, or open and turn their eyes, we say the Judel plays with them. Buy without bearing down the price asked, a new little pot, pour into it out of the child's bath and set it in the over: in a few days the Judel will have sucked every drop out. Sometimes eggshells, out of which the yolk has been blown into the child's pap and the mother's caudle, are hung on the cradle by a threat, for the Judel to play with instead of with the child ... in a lying-in room lay a straw out of the women's bed at every door, and neither ghost nor Judel can get in ... when cows growl in the night, the Judel is playing with them.

The Imprisoned Jew at Magdeburg (see Jew of Tewkesbury)

At the time of Bishop Conrad of Magdeburg, who was born a Count of Sternberg, and who died in the year 1278, a Jew fell into a privy (toilet) on a Saturday. Because it was the Sabbath, the Jews would not pull him out, nor would they allow Christians to do so, because the Jew would have had to help by grabbing hold with his hands. The Bishop was so outraged by this superstition that the following day, Sunday—the Christian Sabbath, he decreed that the Jews would have to keep the Christian Sabbath as well. Thus the poor fool had to spend two days and two nights stuck in a privy.

The Lost Jew (see Wandering Jew)

Once in my life I saw the lost Jew. One afternoon I was home alone when a youthful Jewish man entered my house. He wanted neither to buy nor to sell anything, but with his Jewish accent asked me for a bite of bread. I said to him, "You won't like our coarse peasant bread," to which he replied, "I will like it, if the lady would just give me some."I then asked him, "Have you come a long way?"He answered, "My way is long! I must travel forever throughout the world!" With that he left, but a short time later he returned and asked again for a bite of bread. I immediately said to myself, "Today you have seen the lost Jew," but to make sure I asked the preacher. He listened to my story and said that he could not prove it, but that the belief was there. This answer only strengthened the woman's opinion, which was further verified through an innkeeper's wife from a neighboring village, where the Jew had stayed overnight. She reported that he had eaten nothing and that he had not slept. She had prepared a place for him to lie down, but he paced back and forth in the sitting room the entire night. Even in her old age, the woman who told this story took great pleasure that she had had the good fortune to have seen the lost Jew.

The Magic Ring and the Magic Lock

There was once an old Jew who was a great magician. The magician can raise a mountain but he cannot get at the treasure inside it for the burden of his sin was so great that the mountain would not let him enter. So he finds a peasant lad who performs this task for him. In the mountain, the peasant lad finds precious gems, huge stones which his father wants to sell on his own account. When the peasant lad enters the city, a Jew immediately came up to him and cried. "Farmer anything to sell anything to barter?—Not a lot but something," said the peasant and received more than a thousand for his stones. The Jewish magician tries to get back the magic lock taken from him by the boy. But even the three giants bound to do the sorcerer's bidding express reservations about obeying his commands 'What does the accursed Jew want from us?" say the three giants for they were angry at having to obey the villain.

The Operated Jew (Oskar Panizza 1893)

A young Jewish doctor who seeks to escape his Jewishness (defined as black curly hair, oily skin, thick lips, and a large, hooked nose; posture as orthopedically impaired). He agrees to undergo a series of surgeries. e.g. bones straightening, hair dye (blonde), larynx altered to remove feminine quality and blood transfusion by pure "Aryan" virgins. He then weds a blonde German woman but at his wedding, all previous Jewish features return and degrade into a puddle. The moral? Underneath the most assimilated Jew is the Other, an chimera and non-human.

Pfefferkorn the Jew at Halle

In the year 1515, or according to others 1514, on September 13, the Wednesday following Saint Aegidius' Day, at the Jewish cemetery near Moritz Castle, Johann Pfefferkorn, a baptized Jew from Halle, after having been tortured with red-hot pincers, was bound to a column with a chain fastened around his body in such a manner that he could walk around the column. Burning coals were place around him, then raked ever closer to him, until he was roasted and then burned to death. He had confessed that: 1.For about twenty years he had served as a priest, although he had never been ordained or consecrated. 2.He had stolen three consecrated hosts. He had kept one of them, martyring and piercing it. The other two he had sold to the Jews. 3.Having received one hundred guilder from the Jews, he had sworn an oath to them that he would poison Archbishop Albrecht of Magdeburg and Elector Joachim of Brandenburg, together with all of their court officials. This very nearly happened, for he was in possession of poison at the time of his arrest. 4.Likewise, to give poison to all the subjects of the Archbishoprics of Magdeburg and Halberstadt and to persecute them with arson. 5.He had stolen two children, one of whom he sold to the Jews. He himself helped them to martyr and pierce the one child, so they could collect its blood to mix with their excrement. Because it had red hair, he gave the other one away without harming it. 6.He had presented himself as a physician. However, instead of helping his patients, he gave them poison, thus killing fifteen people. 7.He had stolen a bound devil from a priest in Franconia, using it to practice sorcery. He later sold in for five guilders. 8.He had poisoned wells.

The Jews' Stone/Judenstein (Grimms)(see Blood Libel)

In the year 1462 in the village of Rinn in Tyrol a number of Jews convinced a poor farmer to surrender his small child to them in return for a large sum of money. They took the child out into the woods, where, on a large stone, they martyred it to death in the most unspeakable manner. From that time the stone has been called the Jews' Stone. Afterward they hung the mutilated body on a birch tree not far from a bridge. The child's mother was working in a field when the murder took place. She suddenly thought of her child, and without knowing why, she was overcome with fear. Meanwhile, three drops of fresh blood fell onto her hand, one after the other. Filled with terror she rushed home and asked for her child. Her husband brought her inside and confessed what he had done. He was about to show her the money that would free them from poverty, but it had turned into leaves. Then the father became mad and died from sorrow, but the mother went out and sought her child. She found it hanging from the tree and, with hot tears, took it down and carried it to the church at Rinn. It is lying there to this day, and the people look on it as a holy child. They also brought the Jews' Stone there. According to legend a shepherd cut down the birch tree, from which the child had hung, but when he attempted to carry it home he broke his leg and died from the injury.

The Sun will Bring it to Light.(Grimms)

A tailor's apprentice was traveling about the world in search of work, and at one time he could find none, and his poverty was so great that he had not a farthing to live on. Presently he met a Jew on the road, and as he thought he would have a great deal of money about him, the tailor thrust God out of his heart, fell on the Jew, and said, give me your money, or I will strike you dead. Then said the Jew, grant me my life, I have no money but eight farthings. But the tailor said, money you have, and it shall be produced, and used violence and beat him until he was near death. And when the Jew was dying, the last words he said were, the bright sun will bring it to light, and thereupon he died. The tailor's apprentice felt in his pockets and sought for money, but he found nothing but eight farthings, as the Jew had said. Then he took him up and carried him behind a clump of trees, and went onwards to seek work. After he had traveled about a long while, he found work in a town with a master who had a pretty daughter, with whom he fell in love, and he married her, and lived in good and happy wedlock.

After a long time when he and his wife had two children, the wife's father and mother died, and the young people kept house alone. One morning, when the husband was sitting on the table before the window, his wife brought him his coffee, and when he had poured it out into the saucer, and was just going to drink, the sun shone on it and the reflection gleamed hither and thither on the wall above, and made circles on it. Then the tailor looked up and said, yes, it would like very much to bring it to light, and cannot. The woman said, o, dear husband, and what is that, then. What do you mean by that. He answered, I must not tell you. But she said, if you love me, you must tell me, and used her most affectionate words, and said that no one should ever know it, and left him no rest. Then he told her how years ago, when he was traveling about seeking work and quite worn out and penniless, he had killed a Jew, and that in the last agonies of death, the Jew had spoken the words, the bright sun will bring it to light. And now, the sun had just wanted to bring it to light, and had gleamed and made circles on the wall, but had not been able to do it. After this, he again charged her particularly never to tell this, or he would lose his life, and she did promise. However, when he had sat down to work again, she went to her great friend and confided the story to her, and asked her never to repeat it to any human being, but before three days were over, the whole town knew it, and the tailor was brought to trial, and condemned. And thus, after all, the bright sun did bring it to light.

Germany (Nazi)

After the Nazis seized power in 1933, they called for German folklore that banned folk-alien (international) literature replacing it with "heroic literature"—myths and legends of German and Nordic German racial superiority e.g. The Strongest One Always Wins. Folktales were used selectively for the purpose of creating folkish values, a sort of role model for a folk/Volk personality. For example, censors would delete any reference to pacifism, altruism or peasant stupidity and upgrade it to a warrior status (Kamenetsky, 1992).. By 1938, the Workshop for German Folklore had developed a bibliography that acted as a guide for educators and leaders of Hitler Youth.

The teacher's manual *The Jewish Question in the Classroom* (Die Judenfrage im Unterricht) was distributed throughout the schools of Nazi Germany. The manual begins with "The National Socialist state requires its teachers to teach German children racial theory. For the German people, racial theory means the Jewish problem."—Julius Streicher. Other statements offer testimonials that German children have an inborn aversion to Jews. The teacher's guide suggests that the distorted pictures of Jews are juxtaposed to pictures of the ideal German type. From the visual differences, other differences are inferred. "The Jews walk differently than we do. They have flat feet. They have longer arms than we do. They speak differently than we do."

The thoughts, feelings, and actions of the Jew are presented as a contradiction and threat to German morality. In contrast to the honest German, the Jew is depicted as someone who lives off the sweat of others by his swindling activities In one drawing, the Jewish livestock dealer's attention appears focused on the bag of money; his clothes are tattered and he is ill-kempt. The German farmer, by contrast, although giving the appearance of being exhausted, is adequately groomed. Jesus is viewed as a war hero who waged war against the Jews until he was killed by them. Children were provided with slogans to learn and recite such as: "Judas the Jew betrayed Jesus the German to the Jews." The teacher's guide concludes with a version of world history that implicates Jews in the destruction of major civilizations such as: Egypt, Persia, and Rome. Among several great thinkers, are Hitler's statements against the Jews.

There were three key Nazi folklore books published by Der Sturmer's Julius Streicher and Ernst Heimer. The most poignant example is *Der Giftpilz* (The

Poison Mushroom) where Jews are portrayed as sinister, and ugly while Christians are blond and pretty or handsome. Contrived as a series of lessons, the book likens Jews to deadly wild toadstools, sometimes difficult to distinguish, but always lethal. This first of 17 stories sets the tone for the book. Little Franz and his youthful mother, both blond and dressed in the ideal German country costumes, are out picking wild mushrooms, a popular if risky German recreation. Mother tests Franz to see if he can identify and avoid poisonous mushrooms.

The Poison Mushroom

Just as it is often difficult to recognize poison mushrooms from good mushrooms, so it is often very difficult to recognize Jews as thieves and criminals …

Little Franz went searching for mushrooms in the woods with his mother. Franz, is usually a very quite boy, but today he seems to be transformed. He jumps over bushes and ditches and shouts with excitement. His mother looks on with delight at the happiness of her son. But then she scolds him:

"What's going on Franz? I've already filled up my basket. And you haven't even found one mushroom yet. You've got to be more diligent and look at the ground, not at the sky."

That is how Mother reproached him.

Franz was taken aback. "You are right, Mother. I've completely forgotten to search for mushrooms, it's so beautiful here in the woods. But from now on I'll work harder!"

A half-hour later, Franz returns to Mother triumphantly. "Hurrah! Now I've got just as many mushrooms as you have, Mother. And a bit more quietly he adds: "I think, maybe, there are a few poisonous ones here too." Mother smiles. "That doesn't surprise me! But that's not too serious. We'll just find the poisonous ones and throw them away." Franz takes a mushroom from his basket.

"Mother, this mushroom doesn't look right to me. It's poisonous for sure. Mother nods.

"You've got that right! That's a satan mushroom (boletus satanas). It is very poisonous. You can recognize it by its colour and its disgusting smell." Franz throws the mushroom to the ground and crushes it with his foot. Then he takes another mushroom from his basket. It is big, with a long, light gray stem and a bright red cap with many white spots. "Mother, I don't trust this mushroom either. The color is too gaudy. It must be poisonous too!" "I'll go along with that. It is a fly algaric. Throw it away," Mother confirms. Then Franz presents two other mushrooms from his basket. "But these two are not poisonous. I recognize them. This one is a cap mushroom and the other one is a champignon. You can eat these. They taste very good too." Mother looks at the mushrooms very carefully.

"Correct! We're taking these two home." And she places the two mushrooms in her basket.

"I've got another champignon" Franz calls out and takes another mushroom from his basket.

Mother is suddenly frightened. "For God's sake, Franz! That's no champignon! That's a deadly amanita (knollenblaetterpiltz). It is the most dreadful poison mushroom of all! And it is doubly dangerous because it is so easy to mistake for a good one." Mother now takes Franz's basket and takes out the mushrooms one by one. "That is a chanterelle. It's good to eat, but that one's a sulfur cap (schwefelkopf). It is poisonous. Away with it. And that's a red cap. You can eat that. But this other one is a poisonous saffron milk cap. We mustn't take that home." That's how Mother taught her son about the different kinds of mushrooms. Then they both took their baskets and slowly headed home.

Along the way, Mother said: "Look Franz, just as it is with mushrooms in the forest, so it is with the people on this Earth. There are good mushrooms and there are good people. There are poisonous or bad mushrooms and there are bad people. And you have to watch out for these bad people just like you do for poisonous mushrooms. Do you understand that?" "Yes, Mother, I understand," says Franz. "When you get involved with bad people, bad things can happen, just like when you eat a poison mushroom. It can kill you." Mother asked another question: "And do you also know who these bad people, this poison mushroom of humanity is?" Franz thumped his chest proudly.

"Just as the poison mushroom is often very difficult to distinguish from the good mushrooms, so it often very difficult to recognize the Jews as swindlers and criminals." Yes, Mother! I know that. It is the Jews. Our teacher has often explained that to us in school. Mother laughed and patted Franz on the shoulder. "My word, you are a very clever boy! But now pay close attention so you will understand what I'm going to tell you now. I'll repeat once again: there are good mushrooms and there are bad mushrooms. There are good people and there are bad people. The bad people are the Jews. But it is often really hard to tell apart the bad people from the good ones." "I can understand that," says Franz, "That is often just as hard as sorting out the poisonous mushrooms from the edible ones." "Exactly," Mother praised him. And then she went on. She became very serious. "The Jews are bad people. They are like poison mushrooms. And just as it is often difficult to tell poison mushrooms from good ones, so it is often difficult to recognize Jews as swindlers and criminals. Just as poison mushrooms appear in different forms, Jews also know how to hide themselves, to take on different disguises." "What sort of different disguises do you mean?" asked little Franz. Mother saw that her child had not fully understood. Patiently, she explained further.

"Well, listen carefully. There are, for example, the peddler Jew. With cloth and all sorts of other odds and ends, he goes from village to village. He claims his wares are the best and cheapest. In fact they are the worst and most expensive. He cannot be trusted!" "Just like a poison mushroom. You cannot trust it either." "And it's exactly the same with the cattle dealer Jews (), with the department store Jews, with the kosher butcher Jews, with the Jew doctors, with the baptized Jews, and so on. No matter how they disguise themselves, even when they pretend to be friendly to us, and when they say a thousand times that they mean us well, we must not believe them. They are Jews and they remain Jews. They are poisonous for our people (Volk)." "Just like the poison mushrooms," says Franz.

"Yes, my child! Just as a single poison mushroom can kill a whole family, so just one Jew can destroy a whole village, a whole city, even a whole nation." Franz understood his mother.

Mother, do all non-Jews know that the Jew is as dangerous as a poison mushroom? Mother shook her head. "Unfortunately not, my child. There are many millions of non-Jews who have not learned to recognize the Jews. And that is why we have to teach people and warn them about Jews. We have to warn our youth about the Jews. Even our little boys and girls need to learn to recognize the Jews. They must discover that the Jew is the most dangerous poison mushroom that exists. Just as poison mushrooms shoot up out of the ground everywhere, the Jew can be found in all countries of the world. Just as poison mushrooms often cause the most terrible misfortunes, so too is the Jew the source of misery and poverty, of plague and death."(Afterword) German youth must learn to recognize the Jewish poison mushroom. They must know the danger the Jew presents to the German People and the whole world. They must know that the Jewish Question (Judenfrage) is a Question of Destiny (Schicksalsfrage) for us all. The following short stories report the truth about the Jewish Poison Mushroom. They show us the different forms in which the Jew appears. These stories show us the depravity and baseness of the Jewish race. They show us Jews as they really are, ... Devils in human form.

How One Recognizes the Jew (Woran man die Juden erkent)

In the seventh grade boy's class, things are very lively today. The teacher is talking about the Jews. And that really interests the young fellows. Teacher Birkmann has drawn pictures of Jews on the blackboard. The lads are fascinated. Even the laziest of the students, "Emil the Snorer" is on his toes and not asleep like he often is in other classes. Herr Birkmann is of course a very fine teacher. All the children like him. What they enjoy most of all is when the teacher talks about Jews. And Mr. Birkmann is a master at it. In his life he has gotten to know all about the Jews. And he understands how to describe it all in such an exciting way that the lads like their daily "Jews Hour" best of all. Teacher Birkmann glances at the clock. "It is exactly 12 o'clock," he says. "We are going to sum up what we've learned in this hour. What were we talking about?" All the boys raise their hands. The teacher calls on Karl Scholz, the little whippersnapper in the front row. "We talked about recognizing Jews." "Good, now tell me about that." Little Karl reaches for the pointer, heads for the blackboard and points to the drawings. "The Jews are recognized mostly by their nose. The Jew nose is bent at its tip.

It looks like a number six. It's called the 'Jew six.' Lots of non-Jews have bent nose too. But their noses are bent higher up. That kind of nose is called a 'hook nose' or 'eagle nose.' They have nothing to do with the Jewish nose."

"That's right!" says the teacher. "But one doesn't just recognize the Jew by his nose?" The lad goes on. "One can recognize the Jew by his lips. His lips are usually thick. Often the lower lip hangs down. They're called 'draggers.'

"And you can also tell a Jew by his eyelids. They're usually thicker and fatter . Jews' eyes have a sneaky, piercing look? You can see it right away in his eyes that he is false, lying person."

The teacher calls on another student. He is Fritz Mueller and he is the best in the whole class. Fritz goes up to the board and explains: "The Jews are mostly short to medium height. They have short legs. Their arms are often also very short. Many Jews also have crooked legs and flat feet.

The often have a low, sloping forehead It's called a' runaway forehead.' Many criminals have a forehead like that. And the Jews are criminals. Their hair is mostly dark and often crinkly like Negroes' hair. Their ears are very big and look like the handle on a coffee cup."

The teacher turns to the class. "Pay attention, children! Why does Fritz always say: 'many Jews have crooked legs,' 'often they have sloping foreheads,' 'mostly their hair is dark'?"

Now Heinrich Schmidt raises his hand, a big, powerful fellow in the last row, and explains, "Not every Jew has all these characteristics. Many don't have a real Jewish nose, but they do have real Jews' ears. Some do not have flat feet but do have real Jews' eyes. It happens that at first glance, some Jews can't be recognized as a Jew. There are even Jews with blonde hair. When we want to be really sure that we can distinguish Jews from non-Jews, we have to look very carefully. But when you watch carefully, then you will notice right away if you are dealing with a Jew." "Very good!" the teacher praised him. "And now tell me about the other signs that lets you distinguish Jews from non-Jews. Richard, come on up" Richard Krause, a smiling blond youth goes to the blackboard. And then he gets going: "You can also recognize Jews by the way they move and their bearing. The Jew rocks his head back and forth. His drags his feet and his steps are uncertain. When the Jew speaks, he waves his hands around. It is called 'fiddling.' His voice often breaks when he is talking. The Jew almost always talks through his nose. Often the Jew also has a disgusting, sweetish smell. Someone with a good nose can actually smell Jews." The teacher is pleased. "That's right, children! You have really paid attention! And when you pay close attention like this in the world outside the classroom and you keep your eyes wide open, then you won't be deceived by Jews."

The teacher then presenting a poem on the blackboard for the children to read aloud: From the Jew's face The evil Devil talks to us, The Devil, who, in every land Is known as an evil plague. If we want to be free of Jews and once again seek happiness and joy, then youth must join hands with us, The Jewish devil to conquer.

How the Jews Came to be Among Us (So kamen die Juden zu uns)

In a small old German town. The friendly sun smiles down on the pretty houses and the clean streets. The clock in the town hall strikes the fourth hour of the afternoon. School is out. The school bags on the back or under their arms, the throng of children head homeward. Karl and Fritz are among them. They have arranged to go to swimming together. The water is still a bit cold. But that doesn't matter. German boys aren't softies. The can take it. In the middle of the street, Fritz suddenly stops. He looks at a group of three men. "Karl, just get a sight of that! For God's sake, look at them!" "Oh yes, you mean the three Eastern Jews over there? I know them well. They've been in our town since yesterday." Little Fritz had already seen many Jews. But he had never seen anyone so dirty and ugly. "Why do you say Eastern Jews?" Fritz asked. Karl knows what he's talking about. It isn't for nothing that he is a year older than Fritz and the best student in his class.. "Now, pay attention, Fritz! The Jews we see over there, they come from Galicia or Poland. And because their home is east of Germany, they are called Eastern Jews. Do you get it?" Naturally Fritz understood at once. But he still couldn't grasp it. Just look at those guys! Those dreadful Jew noses! Those beards full of lice! These dirty ears that stick out from their heads! These crooked legs! These flat feet! And these filthy, greasy clothes! And they, they're supposed to be people?" said Fritz. "And what kind of people!" replied Karl, "They are criminals of the worst kind. They lie and cheat, they steal and receive stolen goods. So much nastiness could scare you! At first they start with rags, bones, paper, old furniture and all sorts of junk. Finally they open little stores. They work together with thieves and robbers. Stolen goods go to the Jews and they sell them again. They make a lot of money that way." "And when they've gotten rich from their thievery, what do they do then?" asked Fritz. Karl answered: "When they have enough money, they take off their dirty rags, shave their beards, run away from all this and dress up in modern suits and step about as if they were non-Jews. In Germany, they speak the German language and act as if they were German. In France they talk French and claim to be French. In Italy they want to be Italians, in Holland, Hollanders, in America, Americans, and so on. That's what they do everywhere in the world." Now Fritz had to laugh. "But listen, Karl, that still doesn't help them. Their bent Jewish noses, their Jewish ears, their crooked Jewish legs and their flat Jewish feet, they can't cut those off. That's how you can spot them as Jews right away!" Karl nodded. "Of course you can recognize them when you really open your eyes. But unfortunately there are many people who always fall for the Jewish swindles." "But not me," exclaimed Fritz, "I know the Jews! And I know a fine saying: "From the East they came here once. Filthy, lousy, their purse empty. But after just a few years They became rich. Now they dress themselves in fancy clothes, They don't want to be Jews any more. Therefore eyes open and look carefully: A Jew remains a Jew."

What is the Talmud? (Was ist der Talmud?)

Solly is 13 years old. He is the son of the Jewish cattle dealer Blumenstock from Langenbach. There is no Jewish school there. That's why Solly has to go to the German school. The other students don't like him. Solly is cheeky and impudent. Again and again there are arguments. And every time it is Solly's fault. Today Solly is excused from going to school. He has to go to the Rabbi in the city. A rabbi is a Jewish priest. And this Jewish priest is going to test Solly to see if he has diligently done his Jewish religious studies. Solly has gone into the Synagogue. The Synagogue is the Jews' church. There the Rabbi waits for him. He is an old Jew with a long beard and a real devil-like face. Solly bows. Then the rabbi leads him to the lectern. Here a large, fat book lies open. It is the Talmud. The Talmud is the Jews' secret book of laws. The rabbi begins the examination. "Solly, you have a non-Jewish teacher at school. And you hear every day what the non-Jews say, what they believe and by what laws they live … Solly interrupts the rabbi. "Yes sir, Mr. Rabbi, I hear that every day. But that doesn't concern me. I am a Jew. I obey totally different laws than the non-Jews. Our laws are written in the Talmud." The rabbi nods. "Right! And now I want to hear what you know. Tell me a few of the sayings that you have heard in the school of the non-Jews!" Solly thinks. Then he says: "A saying of the non-Jews goes: 'Work is no disgrace.'" "What are the non-Jews trying to get at with that saying?" "They are trying to say that there is no disgrace when you have to work." "Do we Jews believe that too?" "No, we don't believe that! In our book of laws, the Torah, it says: "Work is very harmful and not beneficial.' "And that's why we Jews do not work and mostly have businesses. Non-Jews were created to work. In the Talmud it also says: 'The Rabbis teach us that there is no meaner work than farming. The Jew must neither plow the field or plant grain. Carrying on a business is much more profitable than working the soil.'" The rabbi laughs. "You have learned that very well. And I know a Talmud saying that you must remember:" Then he opens the Talmud. Solly must read aloud: "The non-Jews were created to serve the Jews. They must plow, sow, dig, mow, bind the sheaves, and grind the flour. The Jews were created to find everything prepared for them." The rabbi continues testing. "Give me another principle or saying of the non-Jews." Solly replies: "The non-Jews say: 'Always be honest and true.' 'Honesty is the best policy.'" "What are the non-Jews trying to say?" "They are trying to say that one should always be honest. One should never lie or cheat. That's what the non-Jews say." "And what do we Jews do?" "We are permitted to cheat and deceive the non-Jews. In the Talmud it says: 'The Jews are permitted to swindle the non-Jews. All lies are allowed.' And it also says: 'Jews are not permitted to swindle his brother. But swindling non-Jews is permitted.'"

"When we loan money to non-Jews, we must set exorbitant interest rates. Because in the Talmud it says specifically: 'It is forbidden to lend money to non-Jews without charging exorbitant interest rates. The non-Jew must receive no benefit from the loan.' Jews are also permitted to rob the non-Jews. In the Talmud it is written: 'Regarding robbery, it is taught: Non-Jews are not permitted to rob each other. The non-Jew is also not allowed to rob the Jew. However, the Jew is permitted to rob the non-Jew at any time.' And it states further: 'If the Jew has stolen something from the non-Jew, and the non-Jew discovers it and demands it back, then the Jew shall simply deny everything. The Jewish court will side with the Jew.'

"In the same way, we Jews are permitted to buy stolen merchandise from thieves if the stolen goods come from non-Jews. We Jews are also permitted to receive stolen goods without committing a sin against our God. Also smuggling and cheating on taxes are permitted. In the Talmud it says that we can cheat the non-Jewish authorities on payments of duty and taxes. It states: 'It is permitted to smuggle because it written: You need not pay what you owe.' And robbery is permitted Jews. But we must only rob non-Jews. The Talmud says: 'The words, Thou shall not steal refer only to theft from Jews, according to the book. It does not refer to theft from non-Jews.'" "What does that mean?" asks the rabbi once more. "That means we are not supposed to lie to or steal from other Jews. But we can always cheat non-Jews. We are permitted to do that." The rabbi is satisfied. "Excellent! Finally, tell me some of the laws in the Talmud!" Solly is happy because the rabbi praises him. He says: "In the Talmud it says: 'Only the Jew alone is human. The non-Jewish people are not called humans, they are classed as cattle.' And because the non-Jews are classed as cattle, we call them 'goy'. We are always permitted to swear a false oath before a non-Jewish court. In the Talmud it says: 'The Jew is allowed to swear a false oath in a non-Jewish court. Such an oath is to be considered a forced oath. Even when he swears an oath in the name of God, he is allowed to lie and, in his heart, to cancel his oath.' Another law says: 'It is written, thou shall not kill. That means one should not kill a member of the Jewish race. However, the goys, the non-Jews are not Jews, so they can therefore be killed.' And it also says in the Sirach: 'Juda, terrify all peoples! Raise your hand over the non-Jews! Stir up the anger of the non-Jews against one another and pour out rage! Smash the head of the rulers who are enemies of the Jews.'"

"That is enough," the rabbi interrupts. He goes to Solly and shakes his hand for a long time. Then he says: "You are a true Talmud scholar. And you will become a genuine Jew. Always think about what the Talmud expects of you. The teachings of the Talmud are our holiest laws. The teachings and laws of the Talmud are more important than the laws of the Old Testament. The teachings of the Talmud are the words of the living God of the Jews. The person who transgresses the laws of the Talmud deserves death. You must think about that as long as you live. When you always obey the laws of the Talmud diligently, then you will join our biblical forefathers in the Jewish heaven. Amen!"

Murder, theft and lies, Robbery, perjury, and cheating To Jewry is permitted! That is known to every Jewish child. In the Talmud it is actually written, what Jews hate, what Jews love, and how they think and live. In the Talmud it is established.

Why Do Jews get Baptized? (Warum sich Juden taufen lassen?)

Anni and Grete are two enthusiastic girls from the Bund Deutscher Maedels[Association of German Girls]. Every Wednesday and Friday, they are "on duty". These are the finest days in the whole week for them. But today, there is no duty day. That's because the Group Leader is ill. Anni is upset. "What are we going to do this afternoon?" she asks Grete."I don't know either!" replies the other girl. And then without another word, the two of them slowly walk into town. The whole day has been spoiled for them. As they pass by the Church of the Redeemer, Grete suddenly halts. "Anni, have a look over there! There goes the department store Jew Veilchenblau with his Rebekka. What on earth do they want here?" Anni smiles. "I know why, Grete! They are supposed to get baptized today." "Oh my God!" exclaims Grete. "Those are some baptismal babies! Just look at the Jew! Crooked legs, flat feet! That nose, that mouth, those ears, that hair! And he wants to get baptized?"

"The Jewess doesn't look any better," adds Anni. "She waddles around like a duck! And her face, I think she stole it from the devil." "Hey, now I know what we are going to do," says Anni. We'll wait here!

We'll see if the baptism has turned Veilchenblau and his Rebekka into non-Jews." "Fine," Anni calls out. "We'll wait."

And the two of them stand in front of the church door.

The clock announces three o'clock. At this moment the church door opens. Veilchenblau and his wife come out. They say goodbye to the pastor. Then they slowly come down the stairs.

"Do you notice anything about the Jews that's become non-Jewish?" asked Anni.

"Not one thing!" whispered Grete. "They still have the same noses and ears, the same legs, the same lips, the same Negro hair! And they waddle around just like they did before!"

Veilchenblau seems to have heard some of the girls' comments. He suddenly stops and shamelessly smirks at the girls-and spits as he passes them. Then he slowly continues on with his Rebekka. The girls look at each other embarrassed.

"What a dirty thing to do! And he pretends that he doesn't want to be a Jew anymore! says Anni.

And Grete cries out: "The baptism has not made him into a non-Jew. And that Rebekka is still a Jew.

Then the two girls head home. But their thoughts are still focused on the Jews' baptism.

"Do you recall," says Anni, "that our group leader once said: 'No more than you can make a Negro into a German, can you make a Jew into a non-Jew!'" Grete angrily stamped her foot on the ground.

"I don't understand the clergymen who continue to baptize Jews. They're just taking criminal riff raff into the church!

"You're right," says Grete. "Despite the baptism, the Jews are still the same crooks they were before. Martin Luther already said that. Popes also said it. And Julius Streicher too!" Anni stood still. Then she spoke and her words were serious and full of meaning:

"I believe that a time will come when Christians will curse the clergymen who let Jews join the churches. Because the Jews just want to destroy the Christian church. And they will destroy it if our clergy continue to accept Jews in the church. As the saying goes:

If a Jew comes running And wants the pastor to baptize him, Then don't trust him and don't do it,

A Jew will always remain a Jew! The baptismal font won't help. Even it won't make the Jew any better! He is a Devil now And remains one for eternity!

How a German Farmer was Driven From his Home and Farm

(Wie ein deutscher Bauer von Haus und Hof vertrieben wurde.)

A hot day in August. Relentlessly, the sun burns down from the sky. No breeze stirs. The heat is unbearable. Even the birds, singing so happily a little while ago are now silent and searching for shelter in the treetops of the cool forest. Only the farmers have no time for rest and relaxation. It is harvest time. The farmer is mowing grain. A sharply honed scythe cuts through the sun-ripened grain, cuts through red poppies and blue cornflowers.

In the background stands the meadow farmer with his wife. And someone else is there too. He is the Jew, Rosenfeld. He has a thick belly. His legs are crooked. And his thick nose is crooked too.

Wildly, he talks to the farmer. With his hands he fiddles around nonstop. And that makes him so hot that sweat pours from his forehead.

The grain farmer doesn't bother himself about the three. He works on diligently. There comes his eleven-year old son, Paul. He brings his father a jug of fresh water. He's got some bread too. Surprised, he glances at the Jew. "Hey, father, what does Rosenfeld want with our neighbor?" That's what the youngster asks.

The father acts as if he did not hear his son and works on. But suddenly he begins to talk: "Boy! That is a terrible tragedy. How often did I warn that farmer! How often have I told him: "Heiner, don't do any business with Jews! But he wouldn't listen to me. He got himself involved with that Jew Rosenfeld. He dealt in cattle with him. Later he borrowed money from him. He signed notes of exchange. And that was the worst thing he could have done.,

The Jew charged usurious interest. Incredible how he cheated the farmer. And now, now he suddenly wants all his money back at once. And now the Jew has mortgaged his home.

The bailiff is coming tomorrow. The farmer, his wife and their seven children will be driven from their home and farm." That is what the grain farmer said. Little Paul is terribly frightened. His eyes spark with rage. "Such a dirty Jew!" he says. And then he is silent for a long time. Full of contempt, he looks at the Jew. He would have liked to smash the water jug over his head. But what could he do, the little fellow! That would not help the neighbor.

"Father, when I grow up, and when I have a farm, then I'll always think about the meadow farmer. And a Jew will not even be allowed in my house. I will put a sign on the door: 'Jews cannot enter!' And if a Jew should try to sneak in, then I'll throw him out at once." The grain farmer nodded. "You're right Paul! Never get involved with a Jew. The Jew just wants to cheat us all the time. The Jew wants to take everything we have. Every farmer has to remember that!" "Yes," said little Paul, "and I'll always think about the saying that teacher told us in school yesterday: The farmer prays to God: Oh, keep the hail away, Protect us from lightning and flood, Then the harvest will be good again. Even worse than these plagues Is the Jew, let me tell you! Be warned: Protect yourself From the Jewish brute!"

The Poodle-Pug-Dachshund-Pincher

The second key antisemitic children's book during the Nazi era was Hiemer"s *The Poodle-Pug-Dachshund-Pincher and Other Logical Narrations* (1937). Hiemer stories links Jews to negative traits in animals. The message is clear—racial interbreding like a poodle-pug-dachshund-pincher creates inferior products. The following examples include

—Cuckoos stealing people's homes to displace the Germans from Germany.
—Hyenas, Jews prey upon disadvantaged Christians.
—Chameleons (the great deceiver)
—Locust (the scourge of God)
—Bedbugs (the blood sucker)
—Sparrows (good-for-nothings),
—Snakes (the viper of humanity, poisonous)
—Tapeworm (the parasite of humanity).
—Bacteria, which threatens existence and must be eradicated.

As young Germans remain under siege by the Jewish plague, Hiemer then concludes exhorts all children to become actively involved in the war against the Jews.

Don't Trust a Fox in a Green Meadow or the Word of a Jew

Of the three children's books, the most widely circulated was *Don't Trust a Fox in a Green Meadow or the Word of a Jew*. Written by 18-year old art student Elvira Bauer, the plot (in storybook style) consists of a fox who schemes to trap its prey, much like The Jew who swears an oath of deceit under the Star of David.

The themes were timely: German vs. Jew, justification for the war against the Jews to save the Aryans. It comes with a warning label—*'Like a fox, he slips about. So you must look out.'*

According to animal folklore, none is more clever and deceptive than the fox. (In Greek legends the fox is the devil.) According to antisemitic folklore, the Devil is the creator of the Jewish people. In an attempt to equal God's creation of humans, the Devil succeeds only in producing unfortunate creatures, among them, the monkey and the Jew. As children of the Devil, therefore, Jews deserve to be ostracized and treated poorly. Their perceived physical and moral defects are regarded as racial characteristics. The positive self-image of the German also has its basis in racial ideology. As contrasted to the Jews, Germans are a pure, healthy race. Bauer alludes several times to what must be done to keep Germany a wholesome. The Jews must be exterminated.

The above illustration points to the intended Nazi solution of the Jewish problem: the expulsion of all Jews from Germany. The sign, followed by a long line of Jewish figures from previous illustrations, reads "one-way street, hurry, hurry" and as a justification for this measure taken against the Jewish population, the second line reads, "The Jews are our misfortune." The word "hurry" and the sentence "The Jews are our misfortune," appear in red, thereby stressing the grave danger that Jews pose to the well being of German society and the urgency with which they must be removed from Germany.

The effect of the circulation of these antisemitic stereotypes among children can be observed in a school composition that was published by Der Stürmer in 1935. The title of the composition is the sentence on the sign in the last illustration: "The Jews are our misfortune." A short excerpt from this composition will suffice to demonstrate the effect of antisemitic propaganda upon the young." Regrettably, there are still many people today who say: Even the Jews are creatures of God. Therefore you must respect them. But we say: Vermin are animals too, but we exterminate them just the same. The Jew is a mongrel Aryans, Asiatics, Negroes, and Mongolian in him." Virtually every sentence of this composition reflects the antisemitic ideas disseminated among young children via propaganda picture books.

Gypsy/Sinti/Romani

Tale of a Wise Young Jew and a Golden Hen

There was once a rich nobleman who had lived with his wife for ten years without having any children. One time he dreamt that he would have a very warlike son. Another time he dreamt again that a Jewess was going to be confined on the same day as his lady. (This was true!) Next morning this lord arose and said to his wife, 'Wife, I dreamt that we are going to have a child.'

'That may really come to pass,' she answered.

He further told her of the Jewess; he said she would be brought to bed at the very same hour as her ladyship.

The good God ordained that she should be delivered of a child; the good God gave them a son. The boy's father was very joyful, as were also the mother and that Jewess, who was brought to bed at the very same hour as this lady.

The nobleman said to his wife, 'My lady, we must go to this Jewess, in order that our child may be brought up with hers.'

'Very well, husband.'

They brought thither the Jewess, and she made her home there, near this nobleman's dwelling.

He begins to grow up, this son of the nobleman. He is very wise; yet the son of the Jewess is still wiser. He is now ten years old, and is eager to go to school; he learns there to perfection. His father and mother are filled with delight.

Once the Jewish boy said to the lord's son, 'Look here, now, why not request your father to have some beautiful baths made for you in the fields?'

The nobleman's son approached his father, kissed his hand, as also his mother's. 'Father,' said he, 'I beg that you will build me some fine baths in the fields.'

Who should it happen to be that set themselves to this work? Two old retainers. They had seen in a town some time before a very beautiful princess. Well, what have they gone and done, these two servitors? They have caused the portrait of this princess to be painted on the walls of the baths. These two servants came back and announced to their lord, 'We have done everything we were ordered to do.'

'Very good. How much now do you ask for it?'

'We shall be satisfied with whatever your grace deigns to give us.'

The nobleman gave them four thousand florins. They accorded to their lord their best thanks. Then the Jew boy called to the nobleman's son, 'Come, the baths are now built, let us see what there is to be seen.'

Thither they went, but this young Jew was always wiser than the nobleman's son. They entered the first hall, where they saw painted upon the walls various kinds of birds, wolves; all which delighted the son of the lord. Then all by himself he enters the other apartment, and what does he behold there? The portrait of this lovely princess painted on one of the walls. He gazes at the likeness of the princess, and is so greatly enchanted with it that he swoons away. The young Jew sees him (swoon); he revives him with vinegar; and he asks the nobleman's son, 'What is the matter with you?'

'O brother, if I do not have this princess to wife I shall kill myself.'

'Hush, for the love of God,' replied the young Jew; 'do not cry so loud. For you shall perhaps have her indeed, only not so soon as you wish.'

He returned home very sick, this nobleman's son.

'What ails him?' asks his father; but the young Jew was ashamed to own what had happened. Orders were given to fetch doctors with all speed; various remedies are administered; but he has nothing the matter with him, for he is quite well, only withering away for the sake of this princess.

'What's to be done with him?' this lord asks himself. He sends the mother to question her son, that he may reveal to her what it is that has happened.

The mother comes to him. 'What is the matter, my child? Don't be ashamed to tell me everything.'

'Ah, mother,' he answered, 'even though I were to tell you all, you would not be able to give me any advice.'

'On the contrary, my son, I will give you very good advice.'

Then he said to her, 'Mother, I have seen the likeness of a beautiful princess in these fine baths; if I do not have her to wife I shall kill myself.'

The mother hears this with delight. 'That is well, my son. In the meantime, where am I to find her?'

But the Jew lad said to the nobleman, 'My lord, I will go with him to seek the princess. I make myself answerable for his person, and if any harm befalls him, punish me.'

'Very well, then; get ready, and set out with the help of God.'

They set out, and on the further side of a large town the young Jew saw a beautiful wand on the road and a little key beside it.

'I shall dismount and pick up that wand,' said he.

But the nobleman's son said to him, 'What good will that wand do you? You can buy yourself a fine sword in any town.'

But the young Jew replied, 'I don't want a sword; I wish to take that wand.'

Well, he got down from his horse; he picked up this wand and the little key. He got into the saddle again, and they went on their way with the help of God. They came to a great forest, where night surprised them. They saw a light shining in this forest.

'See,' said the lord's son, 'there's a light shining over yonder.'

They came up to this light; they went into the room; there was no one within. There they see a beautiful bed, but unoccupied. They see that there is food for them. There is a golden goblet on the side next to the nobleman's son; and beside the young Jew there is a goblet of silver. The nobleman's son would have seated himself beside the silver goblet, but the young Jew said to him, 'Listen to me, brother. You are the son of a wealthy sire, and I am a poor man's son; your place therefore is beside the goblet of gold, and I will seat myself beside the silver goblet.'

Thereafter he disrobed him deftly, and made him lie down on the bed.

'Come you to bed, brother,' said the nobleman's son. 'I don't feel sleepy,' replied the young Jew.

'Well, I'm going to sleep at any rate.'

He placed himself beside the table, this young Jew, and pretended to fall asleep. Two ladies approached the young Jew, but they were not really ladies—they were fairies. 1 These ladies spoke thus to one another, 'Oh! this young Jew and this nobleman's son are going to a capital, where they wish to carry away the king's daughter. But,' said they, 'the young Jew did well to pick up that wand with the little key, for there will be an iron door, which with that key he will be able to open.'

These ladies went away with the help of God. The young Jew undressed himself and went to bed. They arose next morning; they came to that iron door; the young Jew dismounted and opened it. They see that this is the capital wherein dwells the princess. They went into this town; they see a gentleman passing. The young Jew asks him, 'Where is there a first-rate inn in this place?' The gentleman indicated such a one to them, and guided them to it. He paid him for his trouble. They ate until they were satisfied. The nobleman's son remained in the inn, and the young Jew sallied out into the town. He saw a gentleman passing.

'Stay, sir, I have something to ask of you.'

The gentleman stopped, and the young Jew asked him, 'Where is the principal goldsmith's in this town?'

He directed him there; the young Jew went to this goldsmith.

'Will you make me an old hen and her chickens of gold? The old hen must have eyes of diamonds and the young chickens also.'

'Very well.' 'But I stipulate further that she be alive.'

The goldsmith, who was a great wizard, replied, 'Very good, sir; I will do so if you will pay me.'

'I will pay you as much as ten thousand.'

Three days later he returned to get what he had ordered. He chose a Sunday, at the time when the princess was going to church. It was then he proposed to exhibit this golden hen and her chickens in such a way that the princess should see them. Well, he went to the goldsmith's; he got the golden hen with her young chickens. On the following Sunday, he went near the church, this young Jew; he placed a table there, and on it he exposed his golden hen with the young chicks. Nobody who passed that way thought any more about going to church, but all stopped to gaze with wonder at this golden hen with her young chickens. A throng of people gathered from all parts of the town to see this hen and her chickens. The priest himself does not go into the church, but stops before the hen and her chickens; he looks at them so greedily that his eyes are almost starting out of his head. At last the king's daughter comes to church. She looks to see what is going on there. A crowd of people, gentle and simple, gathered together. She had four lackeys with her.

'Go,' she said to one of them, 'see what is going on there.' He went and did not return.

She sent a second one; no more did he come back, so much was he enchanted. She despatched a third; neither did that one return—he was charmed. She sent the fourth, and he returned not either, being enchanted like the others.

'What can have happened there?' she asked herself. 'Has somebody been killed?'

She sent her maid, who forced her way with difficulty among the people; but she also came not back, so much did this golden hen delight her. Another was sent, who with great difficulty forced a passage through the crowd, but she too returned not, so charmed was she. She despatched her third maid-servant, who also penetrated the throng, but, being charmed, did not return. Finally she said to the fourth one, 'I am sending you to see what is happening there; but if you do not come back to tell me, I will have you put to death.'

This one too went. She forced her way after much difficulty through the crowd, but she came not back out of it, so greatly had that golden hen charmed her.

The princess then said to herself, 'What can be going on there? Here, I've sent eight persons, and not one of them has come back to tell me what's the matter.'

Then she went herself to see what had happened. Peasants and gentlemen gave way before her. She draws near and sees—a golden hen with her young chickens.

The Jew lad perceives her and asks her, 'Does this give pleasure to your royal highness?'

'Greatly though it pleases me, sir,' she answered, 'you will not give it to me.'

He took this hen and presented it to the princess; then, with the help of the good God, he went away. But the princess called after him, and invited him to dine at her father's. The young Jew returned to the inn, where the nobleman's son was asleep. He knew nothing of what the young Jew had done. The king sent a very fine carriage to fetch the young Jew; he got into it and drove off. The princess was amusing herself with the hen and its young golden chickens. The king proposed to him that he should live with his daughter.

'Very well,' said the young Jew to him. 'I will live with her.'

Well, they eat, they drink, and at length towards night the young Jew sent some one to fetch the nobleman's son. When he arrived, all three went out to walk in the garden. Then the young Jew said to the princess, 'Will you go away from here with us?'

'Yes, I will go away,' she replied.

They set out with her and hurried away, with the help of the good God. The father of the princess knew not where she had gone to; neither did he know whence the young Jew and the nobleman's son had come. The nobleman's son arrived at his father's house. The father and mother are well satisfied that he has been so successful in bringing home the princess.

'And now, my son,' said his father to him, 'you must marry her.'

So he married her, and they live together with the help of God. The young Jew has also married a wife, and they live together with the help of God.

Holland

According to Jan Ramaekers (1990) the key folkloric themes of undermining were prominent in Holland. Theologically, Jews were viewed as murderers of Christ. Secularized Jews, in Catholic eyes, continued to claim superiority and pursued revolutionary ideologies in order to attain control over the world. Catholic leaders stated that Jews dominated the economic and financial spheres. In the 1930s, the rise of Nazism in Germany prompted some Catholic protests against antisemitism, but also support for it. For the past several decades, Holland has maintained the lowest rates of antisemitism among Christian and Muslim nations.

Hungary

For scholar Peter Hanak (1998) "the Jew represented something anomolous or demonic in which the spirit of witchcraft and destruction dwelt." By the end of the century, as a result of German antisemitic influence, the poor pedlar Jew was depicted as a sinister character with a hooked nose. The clerical satirical journal "Herko Pater" railed against Jews taking over nobles' estates and satirized the Jewish and German accents and manners of speech. The Hungarian nobility, which despised agriculture and trade, formed a negative image Jews as greedy merchants. A survey on the "Jewish question" in Hungary, held by a liberal magazine in 1917, revealed a view of the assimilated Jew as a representative of capitalism and materialism. The antisemitic folklore of Hungary is the roughly the same as Romania and Poland and all regions throughout Eastern Europe. Even within a country however there are variations and twists to the folklore. The following are variations of the Hungarian versions of the Wandering Jew.

A poem version of the Wandering Jew includes a magic flutist and Ahasuerus-Judas character.

> The Ahasuerus worships Mammon (dishonest wealth) and while the magic flutist plays, the Jew has to dance. Eventually he gives money to the flutist in order to silence him. Both fall in love with the king's daughter when they arrive at the Kings court, but the daughter falls for the flutist. The Jew accuses the flutist of having blackmailed him on the way. The flutist is condemned to death but his last wish is to blow his flute. The Jew begins to dance and swears to leave him his fortune if only he stops. Whereby the people hear the verdict and tear the informer to pieces. The magic fluter receives the Jews fortune. (In some versions, the Jew then wanders as a fiddler)

In yet another poem version *A Horribly Wonderful Tale*, the tale continues.

> A rich Jew makes all pecuniary sacrifices for being able to do evil. He makes a coreligionist steal the Host. On Friday in the congregation of Jews, he punctures the wafer which begins to bleed. The terrified Jews run asunder. Two angels descend from Heaven and collect the blood on a gold dish and carry it up to Heaven, The rich Jew turns himself into a wolf and the blood of his heart drops continually and he finds no rest anywhere. He assumes human shape and wanders.

In other variations Ahasuerus is an orthodox Jew on the shore of the Polar Sea unable to die, he tries arrows, wild animals, disease (Cholera) and throwing himself into a volcano. In other versions Moses names him Elias and curses him to roam the earth but as an invisible force.

> In a different elaboration a Jew who converted to Christianity is about to marry a Christian girl. When Ahasuerus/Elijah saw this, he struck the Redeemers sacred image with his stick. A terrible thunder was heard; a dazzling light broke out around the cross. The Redeemers hand hit by the stroke of the stick broke off from the cross made for the Jew and began to thrash him. The Jew cast his stick away and started running. The divine hand persecuted him continually. "Since then, all trace was lost of the godless Elijah, though caters traveling in distant countries assert seeing at night something like a fiery hand flying away and hearing horrible wailing in the meantime. 11

India

It is uncertain if the money-lender designation was Jewish per se since the Christian notion of Jews as money-lenders did not emerge until Middle Ages. Contempt for the money-lender is certain.

There was once a farmer who suffered much at the hands of a money-lender. Good harvests, or bad, the farmer was always poor, the money-lender rich. At the last, when he hadn't a farthing left, farmer went to the money-lender's house, and said, "You can't squeeze water from a stone, and as you have nothing to get by me now, you might tell me the secret of becoming rich."

"My friend," returned the money-lender, piously, "riches come from Ram—ask him."

"Thank you, I will!" replied the simple farmer; so he prepared three girdle-cakes to last him on the journey, and set out to find Ram. First he met a Brahman, and to him he gave a cake, asking him to point out the road to Ram; but the Brahman only took the cake and went on his way without a word, Next the farmer met a Jogi or devotee, and to him he gave a cake, without receiving any help in return. At last, he came upon a poor man sitting under a tree, and finding out he was hungry, the kindly farmer gave him his last cake, and sitting down to rest beside him, entered into conversation.

"And where are you going?" asked the poor man, at length.

"Oh, I have a long journey before me, for I am going to find Ram!" replied the farmer. "I don't suppose you could tell me which way to go?"

"Perhaps I can," said the poor man, smiling, "for I am Ram! What do you want of me?"

Then the farmer told the whole story, and Ram, taking pity on him, gave him a conch shell, and showed him how to blow it in a particular way, saying, "Remember! whatever you wish for, you have only to blow the conch that way, and your wish will be fulfilled. Only have a care of that money-lender, for even magic is not proof against their wiles!"

The farmer went back to his village rejoicing. In fact the money-lender noticed his high spirits at once, and said to himself, "Some good fortune must have befallen the stupid fellow, to make him hold his head so jauntily." Therefore he went over to the simple farmer's house, and congratulated him on his good fortune, in such cunning words, pretending to have heard all about it, that before long the farmer found himself telling the whole story—all except the secret of blowing the conch, for, with all his simplicity, the farmer was not quite such a fool as to tell that.

Nevertheless, the money-lender determined to have the conch by hook or by crook, and as he was villain enough not to stick at trifles, he waited for a favourable opportunity and stole the conch.

But, after nearly bursting himself with blowing the conch in every conceivable way, he was obliged to give up the secret as a bad job. However, being determined to succeed he went back to the farmer, and said, coolly, "Look here; I've got your conch, but I can't use it; you haven't got it, so it's clear you can't use it either. Business is at a stand-still unless we make a bargain. Now, I promise to give you back your conch, and never to interfere with your using it, on one condition, which is this,–whatever you get from it, I am to get double."

"Never!" cried the farmer; "that would be the old business all over again!"

"Not at all!" replied the wily money-lender; "you will have your share! Now, don't be a dog in the manger, for if you get all you want, what can it matter to you if I am rich or poor?"

At last, though it went sorely against the grain to be of any benefit to a money-lender, the farmer was forced to yield, and from that time, no matter what he gained by the power of the conch, the money-lender gained double. And the knowledge that this was so preyed upon the farmer's mind day and night, so that he had no satisfaction out of anything.

At last, there came a very dry season,–so dry that the farmer's crops withered for want of rain. Then he blew his conch, and wished for a well to water them, and lo! there was the well, but the money-lender had two!–two beautiful new wells! This was too much for any farmer to stand; and our friend brooded over it, and brooded over it, till at last a bright idea came into his head. He seized the conch, blew it loudly, and cried out, "Oh, Ram! I wish to be blind of one eye!" And so he, was, in a twinkling, but the money-lender of course was blind of both, and in trying to steer his way between the two new wells, he fell into one, and was drowned.

Now this true story shows that a farmer once got the better of a money-lender—but only by losing one of his eyes.

Ireland

Oisin in Tir Na N-Og(Abridged)

Here was a king in Tir na n-Og (the land of Youth). Saint Patrick had a neighbor, a Jew, a very rich man but the greatest miser in the kingdom, and he had the finest haggart of corn in Erin. Well, the Jew and Saint Patrick got very intimate with one another and so great became the friendship of the Jew for Saint Patrick at last, that he said he 'd give him, for the support of his house, as much corn as one man could thrash out of the haggard [= hay-yard] in a day. When Saint Patrick went home after getting the promise of the corn, he told in the hearing of Oisin about what the Jew had said."Oh, then," said Oisin, "if I had my sight and strength, I'd thrash as much corn in one day as would do your whole house for a twelvemonth and more." Will you do that for me? "said Saint Patrick." I will," said Oisin. Saint Patrick prayed again to the Lord, and the sight and strength came back to Oisin. He went to the woods next morning at daybreak, Oisin did, pulled up two fine ash-trees and made a flail of them. After eating his breakfast he left the house and never stopped till he faced the haggart of the Jew. Standing before one of the stacks of wheat he hit it a wallop of his flail and broke it asunder. He kept on in this way till he slashed the whole haggart to and fro,—and the Jew running like mad up and down the highroad in front of the haggart, tearing the hair from his head when he saw what was doing to his wheat, and the face gone from him entirely he was so in dread of Oisin. When the haggart was thrashed clean, Oisin went to Saint Patrick and told him to send his men for the wheat; for he had thrashed out the whole haggart. When Saint Patrick saw the countenance that was on Oisin, and heard what he had done he was greatly in dread of him, and knocked the strength out of him again, and Oisin became an old, blind man as before. St. Patrick's men went to the haggart and there was so much wheat they didn't bring the half of it away with them and they didn't want it. Oisin again lived for a while as before and then he was vexed because the cook didn't give him what he wanted. He told Saint Patrick that he wasn't getting enough to eat. Then Saint Patrick called up the cook before himself and Oisin and asked her what she was giving Oisin to eat. She said : "I give him at every meal what bread is baked on a large griddle and all the butter I make in one churn, and a quarter of beef besides." "That ought to be enough for you," said Saint Patrick." Oh, then," said Oisin, turning to the cook, "I have often seen the leg of a blackbird bigger than the quarter of beef you give me, I have often seen an ivy leaf bigger than the griddle on which you bake the bread for me, and I have often seen a single rowan berry [the mountain ash berry] bigger than the bit of butter you give me to eat." "You lie!" said the cook, "you never did." Oisin said not a word in answer. Now there was a hound in the place that was going to have her first whelps, and Oisin said to the boy who was tending him: "Do you mind and get the first whelp she'll have and drown the others." Next morning the boy found three whelps, and coming back to Oisin, said: "There are three whelps and 't is unknown which of them is the first." Then Oisin drew out the ivy leaf and asked, "Which is larger, this or the griddle on which you made bread for me?" "That is larger than the griddle and the bread together," said the cook." Right again," said Saint Patrick. Oisin now took out the rowan berry and asked: Which is larger, this berry or the butter of one churning which you give me?" "Oh, that is bigger," said the cook, "than both the churn and the butter." Right, every time," said Saint Patrick. Then Oisin raised his arm and swept the head off the cook with a stroke from the edge of his hand, saying, "You 'll never give the lie to an honest man again."

Italy

Malchus at the Column

Malchus was the head of the Jews who killed our Lord. The Lord pardoned them all, and likewise the good thief, but he never pardoned Malchus, because it was he who gave the Madonna a blow. He is confined under a mountain, and condemned to walk around a column, without resting, as long as the world lasts. Every time that he walks about the column he gives it a blow in memory of the blow he gave the mother of our Lord. He has walked around the column so long that he has sunk into the ground. He is now up to his neck. When he is under, head and all, the world will come to an end, and God will then send him to the place prepared for him. He asks all those who go to see him (for there are such) whether children are yet born; and when they say yes, he gives a deep sigh and resumes his walk, saying: "The time is not yet!" for before the world comes to an end there will be no children born for seven years.

The Story of Judas

When Judas betrayed him, his Master said: "Repent, Judas, for I pardon you." But Judas, not at all! He departed with his bag of money, in despair and cursing heaven and earth. What did he do? While he was going along thus desperate he came across a tamarind tree. (You must know that the tamarind was formerly a large tree, like the olive and walnut.) When he saw this tamarind a wild thought entered his mind, remembering the treason he had committed. He made a noose in a rope and hung himself to the tamarind. And hence it is (because this traitor Judas was cursed by God) that the tamarind tree dried up, and from that time on it ceased growing up into a tree and became a short, twisted, and tangled bush; and its wood is good for nothing, neither to burn, nor to make anything out of, and all on account of Judas, who hanged himself on it. Some say that the soul of Judas went to the lowest hell, to suffer the most painful torments; but I have heard, from older persons who can know, that Judas's soul has a severer sentence. They say that it is in the air, always wandering about the world, without being able to rise higher or fall lower; and every day, on all the tamarind shrubs that it meets, it sees its body hanging and torn by the dogs and birds of prey. They say that the pain he suffers cannot be told, and that it makes the flesh creep to think of it. And thus Jesus Christ condemned him for his great treason.

Buttadeau

> It was in winter, and my good father was at Sacalone, in the warehouse, warming himself at the fire, when he saw a man enter, dressed differently from the people of that region, with breeches striped in yellow, red, and black, and his cap the same way. My good father was frightened. "Oh!" he said, "what is this person?" "Do not be afraid," the man said. "I am called Buttadeau.(He who repels from Christ)" "Oh!" said my father, "I have heard you mentioned. Be pleased to sit down a while a tell me something." "I cannot sit, for I am condemned by my God always to walk." And while he was speaking he was always walking up and down and had no rest. Then he said: "Listen. I am going away; I leave you, in memory of me, this, that you must say a credo at the right hand of our Lord, and five other credos at his left, and a salve regina to the Virgin, for the grief I suffer on account of her son. I salute you." "Farewell." "Farewell, my name is Buttadeu."

Latin America / South America

In *A Short History of Antisemitism* (W.W. Norton, 1976), author Vamberto Morais recounts his childhood experiences with antisemitsm in pre-war Brazil.

> I remember hearing disparaging remarks about the food habits of Jewish families. It was said the children smelled of onions because they took onion sandwiches to school and there was talk of peculiar methods of killing chickens. When a Jew with a long beard appeared down the street, the children would shout, "Here comes the hen-killer! It was said he used to come to Jewish houses to kill the hens according to kosher regulations ... The Jew was funny because he was different ... One of the earliest phases I learned was 'Don't jew the little thing' [don't torment] and one of the first children's books I read was the old morality story of the wicked boy turned good entitled *Tony the Jew.* Jew was therefore a synonym for wicked in Portuguese ... The whole idea of judiacao was intimately linked with the mockery and torments suffered by Jesus. Jewish friends in Brazil have often told me that they themselves use the verb judiar (to jew=to be cruel) and the noun judiacao (ill treatment) without thinking of their antisemitic origin. (Morais, 1976, Pp 2–3)

Anthropologists Singer and Santiago (1991) examined the social transmission of antisemitic folklore among the Maya of Chiapas and Guatemala and noted pre-Hispanic notions of the Sun deity combined with Catholic notions of evil forces as Christ killers.

Jews represent the forces of evil that struggled to kill the Sun/Christ—their central deity—so that the chaos in which Jews thrive could prevail. Jews were destroyed at the end of the First Creation. They perished as humans on earth and they remain as evil supernatural that every now and then—during solar eclipses—attack the Sun trying again to destroy him. Like monkeys—who were also evil human beings destroyed at the end of the First Creation—Jews lead an animal-like existence at eh edges of the earth, i.e. beyond the orderly universe created by the path of the Sun/Christ. (p.20)

Folklorist Nadine Grosser Nagarajan has documented the following metaphor from Argentina.

The Shunned Toadstool

In the past fungi were often regarded with suspicion and fear. Mysterious and magical qualities were associated with their unusual shape and it was also well known that nay of the species could be toxic and even fatal. The fact that they thrive in dark and wet places added to the misgivings people held about them. These weird botanical wonders were given strange names that were supported by folklore and superstition. Even when scientific and rational explanations emerged in time, certain stories prevailed and still appear in their old garb. Myriads of mushrooms spring up all over the world; they sprout, bloom, burst forth and wither very quickly; some of them have become well known for their poisonous deadly attributes, yet others—the edible ones are considered delicacies, fit to be the good of the gods. Most mushrooms have always been treated with great respect for these reasons, but no fungus has been considered as vile and unholy as the edible Auricularia auricula or as it is known by its alternate name Auricula Judae—Latin for Jews ear.

The Auricula grows mainly but not exclusively on dead and dying elders and its nickname goes back to the Middle Ages. People believed that Judas Iscariot, who had betrayed Jesus for thirty pieces of silver, grew desolate and morbid because of his deed, discarded the money and hanged himself on an elder tree. The fungus appeared on the tree as a symbolic manifestation Judas' evil deed as a representation his doomed spirit that cannot find rest. The toadstool is edible, velvety soft and jelly-like and truly looks like a wrinkled disfigured ear. Its vicious reputation does not prevent some people from picking it and consuming it in a stew, despite that it does not seem to add any desirable flavor. Some who like practical jokes might enjoy the surprise and disgust on the faces of their guests when they serve the soup that seems to have earls floating in it.

Hatred and hostility towards Jews was widespread, deep and illogical. People forgot that Jesus himself had been a Jew and that Judas whose exact motives are unknown, had betrayed a friend and not a member of a different

religion or race. Judas' act is but one of the excuses for the spread of discrimi-
nation, prejudice and intolerance. Folklore sometimes as in this case reinforces
the strong negative feelings of those who chose to follow the dark paths. The
unlucky Auricula Judae is regarded as a curse, not just because of its shape but
also due to its repulsive odor that was believed to have some connection with
witchcraft. It grows very quickly and some tales connect its unusual rapid
birth and demise with the full moon and the thundering skies. Thunder is
usually followed by rain and thus creates the ideal breeding field for mushrooms while the full moon exerts a certain additional gravitational pull to
which fungi seem to respond by maturing even faster.

The elder tree shares some of this toadstools despicable reputation since its
flowers and leaves are commonly considered to be foul smelling. The curse fell
on the tree since some say it was its wood that served as Jesus' cross. The legend has been more far-reaching, dismal insinuations. It was believed that God
punished the Jews for Judas' betrayal by inflicting on them the same putrid
smell and some abominable disease. Yet another sinister tale sprang forth as a
result of the previous one claiming that for the Jews the best medicine to com-
bat those illnesses was the blood of Christian children. Thus it became a common conviction that Jews murdered youngsters particularly around Passover.
The proof of the crime—the brownish-reddish flakes that appear on the surface of the baked matzo eaten during the holiday, a sure-sign that blood is
used in its making. (reprinted with permission)

Poland

Researcher Alina Cala has extensively examined Polish Jews and concludes that
social strangeness is a key characteristic. The Jews were suspected of scheming
with the devil having a penchant for witchcraft, lazy and mysterious. The Jew is
an ambivalent figure, a stranger both threatening and serving as a link with the
supernatural world (Bartoszewski, 1984). Cala found four myths which are all
classic as: 1) Christ killers 2) the wandering Jew 3) scab swindler 4) rich swine. As
well, Bartoszewski's (1984) examination of proverbs similarly added different,
dirty, weak, cowardly, rich and miserly, and connected with the devil.

The Christian folk fears Judgment Day Eve for that night the Jewish devil
Chaptur seizes small Christian children. On that night the evil spirits have
power over the Jews drag them out and torment them. That is why on that
night the Jews sing mournful songs. The devil drags old Jews out of the synagogue and throws them into the mud where they suffer until they die. On
Judgment Day one Jew has to be the victim. One was sitting together with
others when he suddenly disappeared. No one knew where he went off to and
no one will ever find him. They do not look for him or weep for him for they

know that the Evil Spirit has seized him. That is why when the Judgment Day approaches, the Jews are seized with fear. Everyone is afraid that this year may be his turn.

If the peasant personally knew the Jews, they did not believe them to be responsible for ritual murder. Such blood libel was instead committed by city Jews—persons unknown to them (Bartoszewski,1984). Other tales tell of Jews as innkeepers, as moneylenders to the peasantry where his religion guides all his actions. Magdalena Opalski documents an 1856 version. where the reader learns,

> This tavern was truly one of those Jewish pits where they lie in wait for the poor peasant's soul—Icek, the local innkeeper, was the humblest sort of Jew, red-haired, lame, [cannily] stupid and evil in the most wretched way. The Jewish Tavern Keeper an his Tavern in 19ᵗʰ C Polish Literature (Jerusalem: Zalman, 1986)

Other tales center on the Nineteenth Century Polish insurrection against the Tzar.

> What is the origin of the name Shebershin? The old people recounted that the town used to have a totally different name. But after much of the kingdom of Poland was occupied by the Russian Tzar, two hundred years ago the Poles revolted against the Russians. Once it was the Sabbath—the Polish insurgents came to the town. On the way they encountered a very observant Jew. The Jew was so pious that on the Sabbath he would not utter a single syllable of profane talk and spoke only in the Holy Tongue. They asked him the name of the town but he did not answer because he did not want to desecrate the Sabbath. They asked him once, twice the same question: "What's the name of this town?" But since he would no longer answer them, they flew into a rage and beat him and slapped him on the face. The Jew, confused and frightened began to cry out. "Shever shin! Shever shin!" [Hebrew: Broken Tooth] Ever since then the town has been called Sherbshin. (Bar-Itzhak, 2001)

Researcher Olga Goldberg-Mulkiewicz explores the role of the Jew in the szopka or children's puppet theater. An analysis of puppet theater implicated the Jew's true nature determined via the New Testament and understanding of the supernatural e.g. Jews explain strange situations and interpret Herod's dreams. The Jew also appears in the scenes that represent contemporary reality, and at times assumes the role of the fellow townsman. Goldberg-Mulkiewicz reports that puppet portrayals of The Jew are at times positive—characterized as healers and good luck charms—"To meet him on the road in the morning brings success the whole day." Yet, there are swift transformations from wise man to a sinister and dangerous clown. Despite the various roles, the anti-Jewish idiom generally falls within the categories of the profane and secular. (see Michlic, 2006)

Romania

In Romania, Jews can be portrayed in a positive light, but like their Polish counterparts, it can all change quickly. For instance, scholar Andrei Ostineau documents the Romanian belief that Jews have higher IQs, but their use of the intellectual gift is merely to advance their nefarious ways through cunning. Jews are religious and family oriented but self-serving "united with each other only" and so on. Romanian antisemitic folklore is first and foremost Christian based, followed closely by a focus on Jews as foreign or strange. Ostineau makes the point that since Jews are not baptized, they are vulnerable to the Devil citing John 8:44 "Ye are of your father, the devil" as decedents of Judas (Judean). Other widespread beliefs include:

—Each year when the Jews take their holiday in Autumn, the Devil must steal one Jew from each synagogue and take them to hell.

—As Jesus was born of a Jewish woman, so she must spawn the Devil. There was a Jewess there who sold devils. A man went to buy and he was shown one in the guise of a big snake and she wanted to know if he was afraid. He said no. The Jewess turned the devil into a frog and when it opened one fierce mouth at him, the man fled and was cured of all his need for it.

—Jews are good luck for Christians. Because the Jew is the devil, evil spirits enter him and not Christians. Christians are spared bad luck as it is absorbed into the Jew.

Other Romanian Beliefs About The Jews

*—*At auspicious occasions such as weddings, it is important to invite a Jew to one's wedding as they ward off evil. Yet, there is no such thing as a good Jew. In terms of vocation Jews are never peasants—they are bank owners, traders and merchants and builders, cart drivers, farmers, jewelers and ragmen. Jews own pubs and position the pubs near churches where at times they have poisoned unsuspecting Orthodox Church parishioners after services. In terms of appearance, Jewish women are elegant, beautiful and good dancers. By contrast, the

men have goat faces with big noses and sideburns (pais). They are physically big people and red headed. Sometimes the Jews are dirty because they were wanderers and they smell because they eat onion and garlic. The Jew's personality is likened to fleas and said to be fearful of dogs and wolves. They are not hunters. They are cowards and make poor soldiers. Religiously, Jews are spiritually deaf and dumb and blinded to Christian ways—"In flacarite" in the flames of hell/ belong in hell. Jews are witches (vrajitor) endowed with magical powers as well.

> Why the Jews have freckles?
> St. Mary went to the cross and Jews cooked a rooster and said "Jesus would reincarnate the rooster, whereby the rooster jumped out of the soul and was alive. However in the process splattered the boiling water onto the Jews and that is how they developed freckles.

> Why Jews do not eat Pork?
> The Jew is a pig and cannot eat himself. Originally the idea was that Jesus on the cross spilled blood on a piglet and Jews couldn't remember which side of the pig the blood splattered so refused to eat any part of him.

> Myth of St. Eli
> God tells Eli to kill the Jews but leave one—Eli kills the last Jew so God punishes him with lightning and thunder why is why it always rains on July 21 St. Eli Day. It is said that Jews can bring rain.

> Myth of Blood Libel
> Jews not only kill Christian children, they kill adults as well in human sacrifice.

Russia

For neo-paganist and nationalist Russians, the 1950s forgery *Book of Vles*, provides a rationale for the separation of the Jewish race from mainstream Russian society. But the more remarkable forgery is *The Protocols of the Elders of Zion*.

The exact origins of the Protocols remains uncertain with speculation that it was plagiarized from French attorney Maurice Joly's satirical essay *Dialogue in Hell between Machiavelli and Montesquieu* (1864). Other evidence from the post-Soviet opening of the Russian archives, suggests that a Russian aristocrat exiled in France Mathieu Golovinski wrote the work for the Tsarist Secret Police. Golovisnski's motivation was to convince Nicholas II that Jews were behind the political unrest in Russia so he would abandon any liberal reforms. The timing of the book is interesting as well. It appears to be written at the convening of the First Zionist Conference in Basel (1897) as Theodor Herzl organized the first formal appeals for a Jewish homeland. The threat of organized Jewry in real life was too much for the folkloric mind to encompass. Consequently the myth of Jews taking over the planet became electric. The Protocols has been reprinted in numerous nations and has numerous reprinting. From reprints for distributorship in Ford dealerships across America to cartoons in Khartoum, the plot is moist and fertile. What do Jews truly think? The Protocols tells us: a group of rabbis are secretly meeting to undermine Christianity and takeover the world. Here is the proof as exhibited by the preface to Protocol One.

1. Putting aside fine phrases we shall speak of the significance of each thought: by comparisons and deductions we shall throw light upon surrounding facts.

2. What I am about to set forth, then, is our system from the two points of view, that of ourselves and that of the GOYIM [i.e., non-Jews].

3. It must be noted that men with bad instincts are more in number than the good, and therefore the best results in governing them are attained by violence and terrorization, and not by academic discussions. Every man aims at power, everyone would like to become a dictator if only he could, and rare indeed are the men who would not be willing to sacrifice the welfare of all for the sake of securing their own welfare.

4. What has restrained the beasts of prey who are called men? What has served for their guidance hitherto?

5. In the beginnings of the structure of society, they were subjected to brutal and blind force; afterwards—to Law, which is the same force, only disguised. I draw the conclusion that by the law of nature, right lies in force.

6. Political freedom is an idea but not a fact. This idea one must know how to apply whenever it appears necessary with this bait of an idea to attract the masses of the people to one's party for the purpose of crushing another who is in authority. This task is rendered easier if the opponent has himself been infected with the idea of freedom, SO-CALLED LIBERALISM, and, for the sake of an idea, is willing to yield some of his power. It is precisely here that the triumph of our theory appears; the slackened reins of government are immediately, by the law of life,

caught up and gathered together by a new hand, because the blind might of the nation cannot for one single day exist without guidance, and the new authority merely fits into the place of the old already weakened by liberalism.

With declared enemies of all none's and such intriguing topics as Brainwashing (#16) the Power of Gold (#22) and Control of the Press (#12) totaling twenty-four topics, the average non-Jew interest was piqued. Like the relationship between the folkloric Jew and the real Jew, here was a folkloric manifesto that told of the real thoughts of Jews. The average anti-Semite needed no further justification or rational—folklore and hate were the perfect combination.

The folkloric Jew in Russia has all the negative stereotypes of Christian/Tsarist Russia (including stranger/other and anti-Christian) but contains the communist/capitalist, dual loyalty appellations as well. The soul of Russia is not a Jewish soul. As in much of Eastern European folklore—the Jew is something nefarious, but the exact reasons are vague or perhaps no longer matter. In the following short story The Jew, all the antisemitic folklore elements of Tsarist Russia come to fore.

From Judaism without Embellishments Tormfim Kichko
(Academy of Sciences of the Ukrainian SSR, 1963)

The Jew

> The colonel smiled, puffed out a coil of tobacco smoke between his moustaches, passed his hand over his grey hair, looked at us and considered. We all had the greatest liking and respect for Nikolai Ilyitch, for his good-heartedness, common sense, and kindly indulgence to us young fellows. He was a tall, broad-shouldered, stoutly-built man; his dark face, 'one of the splendid Russian faces,' straight-forward, clever glance, gentle smile, manly and mellow voice—everything about him pleased and attracted one.'All right, listen then,' he began.
>
> It happened in 1813, before Dantzig. I was then in the E__ regiment of cuirassiers, and had just, I recollect, been promoted to be a cornet. It is an exhilarating occupation—fighting; and marching too is good enough in its way, but it is fearfully slow in a besieging army. There one sitsthe whole blessed day within some sort of entrenchment, under a tent, on mud or straw, playing cards from morning till night. Perhaps, from simple boredom, one goes out to watch the bombs and redhot bullets flying.
> At first the French kept us amused with sorties, but they quickly subsided. We soon got sick of foraging expeditions too; we were overcome, in fact, by such

deadly dulness that we were ready to howl for sheer ennui. I was not more than nineteen then; I was a healthy young fellow, fresh as a daisy, thought of nothing but getting all the fun I could out of the French ... and in other ways too ... you understand what I mean ... and this is what happened. Having nothing to do, I fell to gambling. All of a sudden, after dreadful losses, my luck turned, and towards morning (we used to play at night) I had won an immense amount. Exhausted and sleepy, I came out into the fresh air, and sat down on a mound. It was a splendid, calm morning; the long lines of our fortifications were lost in the mist; I gazed till I was weary, and then began to doze where I was sitting.

A discreet cough waked me: I opened my eyes, and saw standing before me a Jew, a man of forty, wearing a long-skirted grey wrapper, slippers, and a black smoking-cap. This Jew, whose name was Girshel, was continually hanging about our camp, offering his services as an agent, getting us wine, provisions, and other such trifles. He was a thinnish, red-haired, little man, marked with smallpox; he blinked incessantly with his diminutive little eyes, which were reddish too; he had a long crooked nose, and was always coughing.

He began fidgeting about me, bowing obsequiously.

'Well, what do you want?' I asked him at last.

'Oh, I only—I've only come, sir, to know if I can't be of use to your honour in some way ...'

'I don't want you; you can go.'

'At your honour's service, as you desire.... I thought there might be, sir, something....'

'You bother me; go along, I tell you.'

'Certainly, sir, certainly. But your honour must permit me to congratulate you on your success....'

'Why, how did you know?'

'Oh, I know, to be sure I do.... An immense sum ... immense.... Oh! how immense....'

Girshel spread out his fingers and wagged his head.

'But what's the use of talking,' I said peevishly; 'what the devil's the good of money here?'

'Oh! don't say that, your honour; ay, ay, don't say so. Money's a capital thing; always of use; you can get anything for money, your honour; anything! anything! Only say the word to the agent, he'll get
you anything, your honour, anything! anything!'

'Don't tell lies, Jew.'

'Ay! ay!' repeated Girshel, shaking his side-locks. 'Your honour doesn't believe me.... Ay ... ay....' The Jew closed his eyes and slowly wagged his head to right and to left.... 'Oh, I know what his honour the
officer would like.... I know, ... to be sure I do!'

The Jew assumed an exceedingly knowing leer.

'Really!'

The Jew glanced round timorously, then bent over to me.

'Such a lovely creature, your honour, lovely! ...' Girshel again closed his eyes and shot out his lips.

'Your honour, you've only to say the word ... you shall see for yourself ... whatever I say now, you'll hear ... but you won't believe ... better tell me to show you ... that's the thing, that's the thing!'

I did not speak; I gazed at the Jew.

'Well, all right then; well then, very good; so I'll show you then....'

Thereupon Girshel laughed and slapped me lightly on the shoulder, but skipped back at once as though he had been scalded.

'But, your honour, how about a trifle in advance?'

'But you 're taking me in, and will show me some scarecrow?'

'Ay, ay, what a thing to say!' the Jew pronounced with unusual warmth, waving his hands about. 'How can you! Why ... if so, your honour, you order me to be given five hundred ... four hundred and fifty lashes,' he added hurriedly.... 'You give orders—'

At that moment one of my comrades lifted the edge of his tent and called me by name. I got up hurriedly and flung the Jew a gold coin.

'This evening, this evening,' he muttered after me.

I must confess, my friends, I looked forward to the evening with some impatience. That very day the French made a sortie; our regiment marched to the attack. The evening came on; we sat round the fires ... the soldiers cooked porridge. My comrades talked. I lay on my cloak, dranktea, and listened to my comrades' stories. They suggested a game o cards—I refused to take part in it. I felt excited. Gradually the officers dispersed to their tents; the fires began to die down; the soldiers too dispersed, or went to sleep on the spot; everything was still. I did not get up. My orderly squatted on his heels before the fire, and was beginning to nod. I sent him away. Soon the whole camp was hushed. The sentries were relieved. I still lay there, as it were waiting for something. The stars peeped out. The night came on. A long while I watched the dying flame.... The last fire went out. 'The damned Jew was taking me in,' I thought angrily, and was just going to get up.

'Your honour,' ... a trembling voice whispered close to my ear.

I looked round: Girshel. He was very pale, he stammered, and whispered something.

'Let's go to your tent, sir.' I got up and followed him. The Jew shrank into himself, and stepped warily over the short, damp grass. I observed on one side a motionless, muffled-up figure. The Jew beckoned to her—she went up to him. He whispered to her, turned to me, nodded his head several times, and we all three went into the tent. Ridiculous to relate, I was breathless.

'You see, your honour,' the Jew whispered with an effort, 'you see. She's a little frightened at the moment, she's frightened; but I've told her his honour the officer's a good man, a splendid man.... Don't be
frightened, don't be frightened,' he went on—'don't be frightened....'

The muffled-up figure did not stir. I was myself in a state of dreadful confusion, and didn't know what to say. Girshel too was fidgeting restlessly, and gesticulating in a strange way....

'Any way,' I said to him, 'you get out....' Unwillingly, as it seemed, Girshel obeyed.

I went up to the muffled-up figure, and gently took the dark hood off her head. There was a conflagration in Dantzig: by the faint, reddish, flickering glow of the distant fire I saw the pale face of a young Jewess. Her beauty astounded me. I stood facing her, and gazed at her in silence. She did not raise her eyes. A slight rustle made me look round. Girshel was cautiously poking his head in under the edge of the tent. I waved my hand at him angrily, ... he vanished.

'What's your name?' I said at last.

'Sara,' she answered, and for one instant I caught in the darkness the gleam of the whites of her large, long-shaped eyes and little, even, flashing teeth.

I snatched up two leather cushions, flung them on the ground, and asked her to sit down. She slipped off her shawl, and sat down. She was wearing a short Cossack jacket, open in front, with round, chased silver buttons, and full sleeves. Her thick black hair was coiled twice round her little head. I sat down beside her and took her dark, slender hand. She resisted a little, but seemed afraid to look at me, and there was a catch in her breath. I admired her Oriental profile, and timidly pressed her cold, shaking fingers.

'Do you know Russian?'

'Yes ... a little.'

'And do you like Russians?'

'Yes, I like them.'

'Then, you like me too?'

'Yes, I like you.'

I tried to put my arm round her, but she moved away quickly....

'No, no, please, sir, please ...'

'Oh, all right; look at me, any way.'

She let her black, piercing eyes rest upon me, and at once turned away with a smile, and blushed.

I kissed her hand ardently. She peeped at me from under her eyelids and softly laughed.

'What is it?'

She hid her face in her sleeve and laughed more than before.

Girshel showed himself at the entrance of the tent and shook his finger at her. She ceased laughing.

'Go away!' I whispered to him through my teeth; 'you make me sick!'

Girshel did not go away.

I took a handful of gold pieces out of my trunk, stuffed them in his hand and pushed him out.

'Your honour, me too....' she said.

I dropped several gold coins on her lap; she pounced on them like a cat.

'Well, now I must have a kiss.'

'No, please, please,' she faltered in a frightened and beseeching voice.

'What are you frightened of?'

'I'm afraid.'

'Oh, nonsense....'

'No, please.'

She looked timidly at me, put her head a little on one side and clasped her hands. I let her alone.

'If you like ... here,' she said after a brief silence, and she raised her hand to my lips. With no great eagerness, I kissed it. Sara laughed again.

My blood was boiling. I was annoyed with myself and did not know what to do. Really, I thought at last, what a fool I am.

I turned to her again.

'Sara, listen, I'm in love with you.'

'I know.'

'You know? And you're not angry? And do you like me too?'

Sara shook her head.

'No, answer me properly.'

'Well, show yourself,' she said.

I bent down to her. Sara laid her hands on my shoulders, began scrutinising my face, frowned, smiled.... I could not contain myself, and gave her a rapid kiss on her cheek. She jumped up and in one bound was at the entrance of the tent.

'Come, what a shy thing you are!'

She did not speak and did not stir.

'Come here to me....'

'No, sir, good-bye. Another time.'

Girshel again thrust in his curly head, and said a couple of words to her; she bent down and glided away, like a snake.

I ran out of the tent in pursuit of her, but could not get another glimpse of her nor of Girshel.

The whole night long I could not sleep a wink.

The next night we were sitting in the tent of our captain; I was playing, but with no great zest. My orderly came in.

'Some one's asking for you, your honour.'

'Who is it?'

'A Jew.'

'Can it be Girshel?' I wondered. I waited till the end of the rubber, got up and went out. Yes, it was so; I saw Girshel.

'Well,' he questioned me with an ingratiating smile, 'your honour, are you satisfied?'

'Ah, you—!' (Here the colonel glanced round. 'No ladies present, I believe.... Well, never mind, any way.') 'Ah, bless you!' I responded, 'so you're making fun of me, are you?'

'How so?'

'How so, indeed! What a question!'

'Ay, ay, your honour, you 're too bad,' Girshel said reproachfully, but never ceasing smiling. 'The girl is young and modest.... You frightened her, indeed, you did.'

'Queer sort of modesty! why did she take money, then?'

'Why, what then? If one's given money, why not take it, sir?'

'I say, Girshel, let her come again, and I'll let you off ... only, please, don't show your stupid phiz inside my tent, and leave us in peace; do you hear?'

Girshel's eyes sparkled.

'What do you say? You like her?'

'Well, yes.'

'She's a lovely creature! there's not another such anywhere. And have you something for me now?'

'Yes, here, only listen; fair play is better than gold. Bring her and then go to the devil. I'll escort her home myself.'

'Oh, no, sir, no, that's impossible, sir,' the Jew rejoined hurriedly. 'Ay, ay, that's impossible. I'll walk about near the tent, your honour, if you like; I'll ... I'll go away, your honour, if you like, a little.... I'm ready to do your honour a service.... I'll move away ...
to be sure, I will.'

'Well, mind you do.... And bring her, do you hear?'

'Eh, but she's a beauty, your honour, eh? your honour, a beauty, eh?'

Girshel bent down and peeped into my eyes.

'She's good-looking.'

'Well, then, give me another gold piece.'

I threw him a coin; we parted.

The day passed at last. The night came on. I had been sitting for a long while alone in my tent. It was dark outside. It struck two in the town. I was beginning to curse the Jew.... Suddenly Sara came in, alone. I jumped up took her in my arms ... put my lips to her face.... It was coldas ice. I could scarcely distinguish her features.... I made her sit down, knelt down before her, took her hands, touched her waist.... She did not speak, did not stir, and suddenly she broke into loud, convulsive sobbing. I tried in vain to soothe her, to persuade her....

She wept in torrents.... I caressed her, wiped her tears; as before, she did not resist, made no answer to my questions and wept—wept, like a waterfall. I felt a pang at my heart; I got up and went out of the tent.

Girshel seemed to pop up out of the earth before me.

'Girshel,' I said to him, 'here's the money I promised you. Take Sara away.'

The Jew at once rushed up to her. She left off weeping, and clutched hold of him.

'Good-bye, Sara,'I said to her. 'God bless you, good-bye. We'll see eachother again some other time.'

Girshel was silent and bowed humbly. Sara bent down, took my hand and pressed it to her lips; I turned away....

For five or six days, my friends, I kept thinking of my Jewess. Girshel did not make his appearance, and no one had seen him in the camp. I slept rather badly at nights; I was continually haunted by wet, black eyes, and long eyelashes; my lips could not forget the touch of her cheek, smooth and fresh as a downy plum. I was sent out with a foraging party to a village some distance away. While my soldiers were ransacking the houses, I remained in the street, and did not dismount from my horse. Suddenly some one caught hold of my foot....

'Mercy on us, Sara!'

She was pale and excited.

'Your honour ... help us, save us, your soldiers are insulting us.... Your honour....'

She recognised me and flushed red.

'Why, do you live here?'

'Yes.'

'Where?'

Sara pointed to a little, old house. I set spurs to my horse and galloped up. In the yard of the little house an ugly and tattered Jewess was trying to tear out of the hands of my long sergeant, Siliavka, three hens and a duck. He was holding his booty above his head, laughing; the hens clucked and the duck quacked.... Two other cuirassiers were loading their horses with hay, straw, and sacks of flour. Inside the house I heard shouts and oaths in Little-Russian.... I called to my men and told them to leave the Jews alone, not to take anything from them. The soldiers obeyed, the sergeant got on his grey mare, Proserpina, or, as he called her, 'Prozherpila,' and rode after me into the street.

'Well,' I said to Sara, 'are you pleased with me?'

She looked at me with a smile.

'What has become of you all this time?'

She dropped her eyes.

'I will come to you to-morrow.'

'In the evening?'

'No, sir, in the morning.'

'Mind you do, don't deceive me.'

'No ... no, I won't.'

I looked greedily at her. By daylight she seemed to me handsomer than ever. I remember I was particularly struck by the even, amber tint of her face and the bluish lights in her black hair.... I bent down from my horse and warmly pressed her little hand.

'Good-bye, Sara ... mind you come.'

'Yes.'

She went home; I told the sergeant to follow me with the party, and galloped off.

The next day I got up very early, dressed, and went out of the tent. It was a glorious morning; the sun had just risen and every blade of grass was sparkling in the dew and the crimson glow. I clambered on to a high breastwork, and sat down on the edge of an embrasure. Below me a stout, cast-iron cannon stuck out its black muzzle towards the open country. I carelessly about me … and all at once caught sight of a bent figure in a grey wrapper, a hundred paces from me. I recognised Girshel.

He stood without moving for a long while in one place, then suddenly ran a little on one side, looked hurriedly and furtively round … uttered a cry, squatted down, cautiously craned his neck and began looking round again and listening. I could see all his actions very clearly. He put his hand into his bosom, took out a scrap of paper and a pencil, and began writing or drawing something. Girshel continually stopped, started like a hare, attentively scrutinised everything around him, and seemed to be sketching our camp. More than once he hid his scrap of paper, half closed his eyes, sniffed at the air, and again set to work. At last, the Jew squatted down on the grass, took off his slipper, and stuffed the paper in it; but he had not time to regain his legs, when suddenly, ten steps from him, there appeared from behind the slope of an earthwork the whiskered countenance of the sergeant Siliavka, and gradually the whole of his long clumsy figure rose up from the ground. The Jew stood with his back to him. Siliavka went quickly up to him and laid his heavy paw on his shoulder. Girshel seemed to shrink into himself. He shook like a leaf and uttered a feeble cry, like a hare's. Siliavka addressed him threateningly, and seized him by the collar. I could not hear their conversation, but from the despairing gestures of the Jew, and his

supplicating appearance, I began to guess what it was. The Jew twice flung himself at the sergeant's feet, put his hand in his pocket, pulled out a torn check handkerchief, untied a knot, and took out gold

coins.… Siliavka took his offering with great dignity, but did not leave off dragging the Jew by the collar. Girshel made a sudden bound and rushed away; the sergeant sped after him in pursuit. The Jew ran

exceedingly well; his legs, clad in blue stockings, flashed by, really very rapidly; but Siliavka after a short run caught the crouching Jew, made him stand up, and carried him in his arms straight to the camp. I got up and went to meet him.

'Ah! your honour!' bawled Siliavka,—'it's a spy I'm bringing you—a spy! …' The sturdy Little-Russian was streaming with perspiration. 'Stop that wriggling, devilish Jew—now then … you wretch! you'd better look out, I'll throttle you!'

The luckless Girshel was feebly prodding his elbows into Siliavka's chest, and feebly kicking.… His eyes were rolling convulsively.…

'What's the matter?' I questioned Siliavka.

'If your honour'll be so good as to take the slipper off his right foot,—I can't get at it.' He was still holding the Jew in his arms.

I took off the slipper, took out of it a carefully folded piece of paper, unfolded it, and found an accurate map of our camp. On the margin were a number of notes written in a fine hand in the Jews' language.

Meanwhile Siliavka had set Girshel on his legs. The Jew opened his eyes, saw me, and flung himself on his knees before me.

Without speaking, I showed him the paper.

'What's this?'

'It's—nothing, your honour. I was only.... ' His voice broke.

'Are you a spy?'

He did not understand me, muttered disconnected words, pressed my knees in terror....

'Are you a spy?'

'I!' he cried faintly, and shook his head. 'How could I? I never did; I'm not at all. It's not possible; utterly impossible. I'm ready—I'll—this minute—I've money to give ... I'll pay for it,' he whispered, and closed his eyes.

The smoking-cap had slipped back on to his neck; his reddish hair was soaked with cold sweat, and hung in tails; his lips were blue, and working convulsively; his brows were contracted painfully; his face was drawn....

Soldiers came up round us. I had at first meant to give Girshel a good fright, and to tell Siliavka to hold his tongue, but now the affair had become public, and could not escape 'the cognisance of the authorities.'

'Take him to the general,' I said to the sergeant.

'Your honour, your honour!' the Jew shrieked in a voice of despair. 'I am not guilty ... not guilty.... Tell him to let me go, tell him ...'

'His Excellency will decide about that,' said Siliavka. 'Come along.'

'Your honour!' the Jew shrieked after me—'tell him! have mercy!'

His shriek tortured me; I hastened my pace. Our general was a man of German extraction, honest and good-hearted, but strict in his adherence to military discipline. I went into the little house that had been hastily put up for him, and in a few words explained the reason of my visit. I knew the severity of the military regulations, and so I did not even pronounce the word 'spy,' but tried to put the whole affair before him as something quite trifling and not worth attention. But, unhappily for Girshel, the general put doing his duty higher than pity.

'You, young man,' he said to me in his broken Russian, 'inexperienced are. You in military matters yet inexperienced are. The matter, of which you to me reported have, is important, very important.... And where is this man who taken was? This Jew? where is he?'

I went out and told them to bring in the Jew. They brought in the Jew. The wretched creature could scarcely stand up.

'Yes,' pronounced the general, turning to me; 'and where's the plan which on this man found was?'

I handed him the paper. The general opened it, turned away again, screwed up his eyes, frowned....

'This is most as-ton-ish-ing ... ' he said slowly. 'Who arrested him?'

'I, your Excellency!' Siliavka jerked out sharply.

'Ah! good! good! ... Well, my good man, what do you say in your defence?'

'Your ... your ... your Excellency,' stammered Girshel, 'I ... indeed, ... your Excellency ... I'm not guilty ... your Excellency; ask his honour the officer.... I'm an agent, your Excellency, an honest agent.'

'He ought to be cross-examined,' the general murmured in an undertone, wagging his head gravely. 'Come, how do you explain this, my friend?' 'I'm not guilty, your Excellency, I'm not guilty.'

'That is not probable, however. You were—how is it said in Russian?—taken on the fact, that is, in the very facts!'

'Hear me, your Excellency; I am not guilty.'

'You drew the plan? you are a spy of the enemy?'

'It wasn't me!' Girshel shrieked suddenly; 'not I, your Excellency!'

The general looked at Siliavka.

'Why, he's raving, your Excellency. His honour the officer here took the plan out of his slipper.'

The general looked at me. I was obliged to nod assent.

'You are a spy from the enemy, my good man....'

'Not I ... not I ... ' whispered the distracted Jew.

'You have the enemy with similar information before provided? Confess....'

'How could I?'

'You will not deceive me, my good man. Are you a spy?'

The Jew closed his eyes, shook his head, and lifted the skirts of his gown.

'Hang him,' the general pronounced expressively after a brief silence,'according to the law. Where is Mr. Fiodor Schliekelmann?'

They ran to fetch Schliekelmann, the general's adjutant. Girshel began to turn greenish, his mouth fell open, his eyes seemed starting out of his head. The adjutant came in. The general gave him the requisite
instructions. The secretary showed his sickly, pock-marked face for an instant. Two or three officers peeped into the room inquisitively.

'Have pity, your Excellency,' I said to the general in German as best I could; 'let him off....'

'You, young man,' he answered me in Russian, 'I was saying to you, are inexperienced, and therefore I beg you silent to be, and me no more to trouble.'

Girshel with a shriek dropped at the general's feet.

'Your Excellency, have mercy; I will never again, I will not, your Excellency; I have a wife ... your Excellency, a daughter ... have mercy....'

'It's no use!'

'Truly, your Excellency, I am guilty ... it's the first time, your Excellency, the first time, believe me!'

'You furnished no other documents?'

'The first time, your Excellency, … my wife … my children … have mercy.…'

'But you are a spy.'

'My wife … your Excellency … my children.…'

The general felt a twinge, but there was no getting out of it.

'According to the law, hang the Hebrew,' he said constrainedly, with the air of a man forced to do violence to his heart, and sacrifice his better feelings to inexorable duty—'hang him! Fiodor Karlitch, I beg
you to draw up a report of the occurrence.…'

A horrible change suddenly came over Girshel. Instead of the ordinary timorous alarm peculiar to the Jewish nature, in his face was reflected the horrible agony that comes before death. He writhed like a wild beast trapped, his mouth stood open, there was a hoarse rattle in his throat, he positively leapt up and down, convulsively moving his elbows. He had on only one slipper; they had forgotten to put the other on again … his gown fell open … his cap had fallen off.…

We all shuddered; the general stopped speaking.

'Your Excellency,' I began again, 'pardon this wretched creature.'

'Impossible! It is the law,' the general replied abruptly, and not without emotion, 'for a warning to others.'

'For pity's sake.…'

'Mr. Cornet, be so good as to return to your post,' said the general, and he motioned me imperiously to the door.

I bowed and went out. But seeing that in reality I had no post anywhere, I remained at no great distance from the general's house.

Two minutes later Girshel made his appearance, conducted by Siliavka and three soldiers. The poor Jew was in a state of stupefaction, and could hardly move his legs. Siliavka went by me to the camp, and soon returned with a rope in his hands. His coarse but not ill-natured face wore a look of strange, exasperated commiseration. At the sight of the rope the Jew flung up his arms, sat down, and burst into sobs. The soldiers stood silently about him, and stared grimly at the earth. I went up to Girshel, addressed him; he sobbed like a baby, and did not even look at me. With a hopeless gesture I went to my tent, flung myself on a rug, and closed my eyes....

Suddenly some one ran hastily and noisily into my tent. I raised my head and saw Sara; she looked beside herself. She rushed up to me, and clutched at my hands.

'Come along, come along,' she insisted breathlessly.

'Where? what for? let us stop here.'

'To father, to father, quick ... save him ... save him!'

'To what father?'

'My father; they are going to hang him....'

'What! is Girshel ...?'

'My father ... I'll tell you all about it later,' she added, wringingher hands in despair: 'only come ... come....'

We ran out of the tent. In the open ground, on the way to a solitary birch-tree, we could see a group of soldiers.... Sara pointed to them without speaking....

'Stop,' I said to her suddenly: 'where are we running to? The soldiers won't obey me.'

Sara still pulled me after her.... I must confess, my head was going round.

'But listen, Sara,' I said to her; 'what sense is there in running here? It would be better for me to go to the general again; let's go together; who knows, we may persuade him.'

Sara suddenly stood still and gazed at me, as though she were crazy.

'Understand me, Sara, for God's sake. I can't do anything for your father, but the general can. Let's go to him.'

'But meanwhile they'll hang him,' she moaned....

I looked round. The secretary was standing not far off.

'Ivanov,' I called to him; 'run, please, over there to them, tell them to wait a little, say I've gone to petition the general.'

'Yes, sir.'

Ivanov ran off.

We were not admitted to the general's presence. In vain I begged, persuaded, swore even, at last ... in vain, poor Sara tore her hair and rushed at the sentinels; they would not let us pass.

Sara looked wildly round, clutched her head in both hands, and ran at breakneck pace towards the open country, to her father. I followed her. Every one stared at us, wondering.

We ran up to the soldiers. They were standing in a ring, and picture it, gentlemen! they were laughing, laughing at poor Girshel. I flew into a rage and shouted at them. The Jew saw us and fell on his daughter's neck. Sara clung to him passionately.

The poor wretch imagined he was pardoned.... He was just beginning to thank me ... I turned away.

'Your honour,' he shrieked and wrung his hands; 'I'm not pardoned?'

I did not speak.

'No?'

'No.'

'Your honor,' he began muttering; 'look, your honor, look ... she, this girl, see—you know—she's my daughter.'

'I know,' I answered, and turned away again.

'Your honor,' he shrieked, 'I never went away from the tent! I wouldn't for anything ...'

He stopped, and closed his eyes for an instant.... 'I wanted your money, your honor, I must own ... but not for anything....'

I was silent. Girshel was loathsome to me, and she too, his accomplice....

'But now, if you save me,' the Jew articulated in a whisper, 'I'll command her
... I ... do you understand? ... everything ... I'll go to every length....'

He was trembling like a leaf, and looking about him hurriedly. Sara silently
and passionately embraced him.

The adjutant came up to us.

'Cornet,' he said to me; 'his Excellency has given me orders to place you under
arrest. And you ... ' he motioned the soldiers to the Jew ... 'quickly.'

Siliavka went up to the Jew.

'Fiodor Karlitch,' I said to the adjutant (five soldiers had come with him); 'tell
them, at least, to take away that poor girl....'

'Of course. Certainly.'

The unhappy girl was scarcely conscious. Girshel was muttering something to
her in Yiddish....

The soldiers with difficulty freed Sara from her father's arms, and carefully
carried her twenty steps away. But all at once she broke from their arms and
rushed towards Girshel.... Siliavka stopped her. Sara pushed him away; her
face was covered with a faint flush, her eyes flashed, she stretched out her
arms.

'So may you be accursed,' she screamed in German; 'accursed, thrice accursed,
you and all the hateful breed of you, with the curse of Dathan and Abiram,
the curse of poverty and sterility and violent, shameful death! May the earth
open under your feet, godless, pitiless, bloodthirsty dogs....'

Her head dropped back ... she fell to the ground.... They lifted her up and
carried her away.

The soldiers took Girshel under his arms. I saw then why it was they had been
laughing at the Jew when I ran up from the camp with Sara. He was really
ludicrous, in spite of all the horror of his position. The
intense anguish of parting with life, his daughter, his family, showed itself in
the Jew in such strange and grotesque gesticulations, shrieks, and wriggles that
we all could not help smiling, though it was
horrible—intensely horrible to us too. The poor wretch was half dead with
terror....

'Oy! oy! oy!' he shrieked: 'oy … wait! I've something to tell you … a lot to tell you. Mr. Under-sergeant, you know me. I'm an agent, an honest agent. Don't hold me; wait a minute, a little minute, a tiny

minute—wait! Let me go; I'm a poor Hebrew. Sara … where is Sara? Oh, I know, she's at his honour the quarter-lieutenant's.' (God knows why he bestowed such an unheard-of grade upon me.) 'Your honour the quarter-lieutenant, I'm not going away from the tent.' (The soldiers were taking hold of Girshel … he uttered a deafening shriek, and wriggled out of their hands.) 'Your Excellency, have pity on the unhappy

father of a family. I'll give you ten golden pieces, fifteen I'll give, your Excellency! … ' (They dragged him to the birch-tree.) 'Spare me! have mercy! your honour the quarter-lieutenant! your Excellency, the general and commander-in-chief!'

They put the noose on the Jew…. I shut my eyes and rushed away.

I remained for a fortnight under arrest. I was told that the widow of the luckless Girshel came to fetch away the clothes of the deceased. The general ordered a hundred roubles to be given to her. Sara I never saw again. I was wounded; I was taken to the hospital, and by the time I was well again, Dantzig had surrendered, and I joined my regiment on the banks of the Rhine.

—from The Jew and Other Stories by Ivan Sergeevich Turgenev
http://www.gutenberg.org/catalog/world/readfile?fk_files=18430&pageno=17
… 'Tell us a story, colonel,' we said at last to Nikolai Ilyitch.

Scandinavia

There is no known antisemitic folklore of Iceland, Sweden, Norway and Denmark. What is interesting is that there may be folkloric equivalents. The analogue of Jews in Scandinavia may be the trolls who are known for their "cunning and deceitful" ways. These trolls live in the forestlands, are generally not attractive and when they are interchangeable with giants (jotner, jättar or jætter), they live even farther from society because they can't stand the sound of church bells. Jews could also be represented by dwarves (or dark/black elves) a race that lives on as Wights (vättar or huldrefolk)—though Wights live underground, often right next to human settlements, and are commonly a menace to their ground-dwelling neighbors.

Serbia

According to Ljubica Stefan's *From Fairy Tale to Holocaust* (1993), Serbian linguist Vuk Stefanovic Karadzic, compiled Serbian Folktales in 1853. The story called "The Yids" paralled "Hansel and Gretel", substituting Jews for the Wicked Witch who would chase Christian children and devour them.

> Then there came along some Yids, and when they saw the fire, came up to the children and asked them what they were doing there and whether there was anyone with them, and when the children had told them what and how, the Yids told them to go along with them, saying that they would have a fine time at their house. The children agreed and went with the Yids, and the Yids took them to their house. They didn't have anyone else at home, only their mother, and when they came home, they shut the boy up to get fat and made the girl a servant to their mother. One day, when the boy had been well fed and was fat, the Yids went out on some errand and told their mother to roast him, and then when they came home in the evening from their work, they would eat him ...

Slovakia

As in Poland the central image of the Jew is "strange." In Slovkian folklore the gypsy/Romani are deemed the Other and the Jew is just considered strange. The strangeness is mysterious and more apt to be misunderstanding. The term itself Jew can describe an innkeeper or merchant and the opposite all things Christian—emotionless, uncaring, avaricious. Jew can also be used as a curse word.

> Traveling across the world, Jesus Christ hired a Ruthenian, a Magyar and a Jew and told them to come below the village in the morning. The Ruthenian knit a krpce (Peasant Boot) all night, the Jew bandaged his had with a scarf and started to sway, had a breakfast and only then he went to work. The Magyar, a Calvinist, got up in the morning, took bread and bacon and went to work. He came first, greeted "God Bless You" and gave him a fertile fishy land. The Ruthenian was the second to come, God told him that the Magyar had already received the happiness, he gave him infertile land where he had to work hard and even help the Calvinist. The Jew was the last.: the Magyar had happiness, the Ruthenian had hard work to do, and the Jew only swindling; he bought matches, needles, various papers, colors, ribbons, knives and went from village to village to lie to people.

Slovenia

According to researcher Hannah Starman (2004), Jews in modern Slovenia are marked by their non-presence. The antisemitic myths are consistent with Eastern Europe legends portraying The Jews behaving in undermining ways.

South Africa

As Europeans moved to colonize Africa, they packed antisemitism in the suitcase. In the 1870's South African antisemitism began with the myth of 'the plotting Jew,' perhaps stemming from the influx of Lithuanian immigrants and their quick success. The Dutch imported commonly held ideas of Jews as 'knave, dishonest cunning and devious.' The image of the crooked cosmopolitan Jewish financier (exemplified by the characters of "Hoggenheimer" and "Goldenstein" in drama and cartoons) became embedded in South African ethnic mythology. They were held to be physically repulsive. References to the 'Israelitish Boereverneukers' (peasant fuckers) mixed with biblical passages of 'stiff necked' or perverse. With increased financial competition their name changed to Peruvians, and carried a negative connotation (Shain, 1984).

Spain

In Western Europe, Spain has consistently the highest rates of antisemitism (Holland, Scandinavia and the United States has the lowest) superceded by higher rates in Russia and rates that are doubled in Arab Muslim nations. Spain also has the most antisemitic festivals (see Appendix). Whether or not Spain has the most antisemitic folklore is not known, but there is a statistical correlation between superstition belief and antisemitism (Baum & Rudski, 2008). The following tales are from Spain.

A Medieval Antisemite

> In the fourth year of the reign of the great King Alfonso of Spain on the eve of the Jewish passover, 3 miscreants, enemies of Israel as the dead body of a Christian into the house of a Jew and immediately hastened to inform the authorities that the latter had killer a Christian. The Jew was arrested and during the night, the Christians attacked the Jews and killed many of them but some found shelter in the houses of the nobles. The rumor spread to Palma where similar scenes took place. In their hour of distress, the Jews sent a depu-

tation of 3 prominent men to the King imploring his justice and protection. The King issued a proclamation promising a big reward to anyone who would bring information concerning the murder. The effect was immediate The valet of Juan de Vera presented himself before the authorities and informed them that his master was responsible for the murder. He had had some quarrel wit the Jew in whose house the dead body of the Christian had been found and one day said to him: Go and kill that swine of a Jew and I will give thee a silk garment and 20 pieces of gold' but he had refused the bribe. Thereupon, continued the valet 'my master called in 6 of his neighbors and thus he spoke to them: "The Jews have crucified our Savior and it would be a deed agreeable to God to kill them If the King protects them he does it simply out of self-interest on account of the money they are giving him." The conspirators, continued the valet "opened a freshly dug grave and dragging away the body that had only recently been buried carried it off and cast it into the house of the Jew. In order to hide all the traces of their theft and avoid any suspicion which might arise on account of the empty grave, they threw a big stone into it and covered it up." Thus spoke the valet and his master Juan de Vera was immediately summoned into the presence of the King and his judges. The accused at first tried to deny the truth of his valet's words, but when the grave was opened and the big stone found therein, he preened that it was the Jew himself who had stolen the dead body and placed the stone in the empty grave. Witnesses however, now came along and related that they had seen Juan de Vera carry a dead body in the night but had paid no attention to the incident at the time and the calumniator was condemned to death. (Rappoport, 1937/1972)

The God-fearing Sultan and the Prophet Elijah,

Jews are again threatened to be killed—this time by The Grand Vizier, repeating each night to Sultan Solyman "Arise and destroy the people of Israel in they realm for such is the will of God and His command! Elijah the prophet shows up in the nick of time and convinces the Sultan that his vizier has been devious. In the end, "The miscreant who had planned to destroy the Jews was hanged in from of his own house and the incident was written down in the chronicles of the realm to serve as a warning to all future enemies of the Jews." As a reward for his justice, the prophet continued to visit the Sultan from time to time. (Rappoport, 1937/1972)

King's Parade

In Zaragoza, (Saragossa Spain) the capital city, the large Jewish community took the opportunity of showing the King of Aragon their appreciation. Whenever the king celebrated some special occasion with a royal parade which passed through the Jewish quarter, the leaders of the Jewish community would go forth to meet him, carrying the beautiful cases which housed their Sifrei Torah (Torah Scrolls). The actual Sifrei Torah they would leave behind in the synagogues. All this show of honor pleased the king mightily, and all would have been well had there not been a man in the king's court who hated the Jews and resented the king's friendly feelings towards them. This man's name was Marcus, and he looked for a way of putting the Jews in a bad light and at the same time, gaining favor for himself. When by chance Marcus learned that the Jews went to meet the king carrying empty cases, leaving the holy Sifrei Torah behind in the synagogues, he felt he had found the opportunity he was looking for, and told the king about it. The king, not a malicious but neither a very clever man, was easily convinced by the sly Marcus that the Jews meant to mock him by carrying empty cases when they went out to greet him at his parades. Seeing how angry he had managed to make the king against the Jews, Marcus quickly suggested that the king give an order to have all the Jews driven out of the land or killed. However angry the King of Aragon was he had not intended doing anything so dreadful to the Jews by way of punishment, so he said:"I understand they have a powerful God. Would He not punish me for hurting His people?" "The Jews cannot expect mercy or consideration from their God. Since they live comfortably under your reign, they have drifted away from their religion and do not obey His commandments," said Marcus with conviction. "But if we send the Jews out of our land won't our country suffer? After all, they pay taxes and are useful citizens." "The Jews are really so scattered about the land that you wouldn't notice their absence very much," urged Marcus. "But is it fair to punish all the Jews? What about those who are innocent?" feebly protested the king. "Your Majesty should know that they are all the same. They all stick together in all they do, and so they are all equally to blame for the disrespect they have shown you. Besides, it is the heads of the community who come out to greet you in the procession, so surely there is no excuse for them," finished Marcus, with a smile on his face, feeling sure he had won the argument."Look here Marcus, I am indeed very angry with the Jews and agree that they must be severely punished, if what you say is true. But I want to be fair to them, for they have so far always shown themselves to be loyal subjects. At the next parade, when the Jews come out to meet me, I'll have you riding by my side. I give you the authority to open their holy cases and, if they are found to be empty, you may carry out your plan against them. On the other hand, if what you say is untrue, then the punishment will be turned against yourself. Are you prepared to accept that? I do not intend to be made a fool of by anyone." Marcus, who was quite sure that he had the right information, readily agreed. He was already picturing himself riding beside the king, sitting beside the king, and being second to the king in everything. The night before the royal parade, the shamash (beadle) of the main Jewish congregation in Zaragoza could not fall asleep. He was thinking about the king's visit to the Jewish quarter, and he was worried. He tossed and turned and was weighed down by a dreadful feeling that something terrible was threatening the Jewish community. He felt an urge to run out and warn the heads of the community, but thought that they would laugh at him, for everything was so nice and peaceful for them. Finally he fell into an uneasy sleep. He dreamt that an old, gray-bearded, stately man appeared before him, saying: "Arise! Waste no time. Danger threatens the Jews. Hurry to the synagogue and quickly put the Sifrei Torah inside their cases. But say not a word to anyone!" Before the shamash had a chance to say anything, the vision disappeared. He quickly awoke, trembling with fright. He pulled on some clothes and ran all the way to the Synagogue, stumbling in the dark. He was certain that the man in his dream must be none other than Elijah the Prophet, and that his dream was a serious warning which he must see to without delay. What the shamash did not know was that he was not the only one to whom the prophet had appeared. All the other Synagogue beadles in the city of Zaragoza had the same dream that night. They had likewise hurried to their synagogues and secretly put the Sifrei Torah inside their cases, anxiously awaiting developments. The following morning, the sound of the trumpets was heard in the city, heralding the beginning of the royal parade. As always, the heads of the Jewish community went out to meet the king. As the royal carriage stopped for the king to receive the greetings of the heads of the Jewish community, Marcus, who was sitting by the side of the king said:"Your Majesty surely wishes to see what is inside these things that the Jews are carrying." "Of course. Open the cases!" ordered the king.

The Jews were horrified at the unexpected request. What would the king say, or do? They had no choice but to obey, so, with sinking hearts they opened up the cases and, to their wonderment and relief beheld the Sifrei Torah inside, for all to see. The king seemed quite surprised. As for Marcus, the look of expectancy and triumph disappeared from his face, which had now turned pale with fright. He tried to speak, but no words came. Instead, the king burst upon him in rage. "Traitor! Deceiver! This time you have outsmarted yourself and you shall suffer the penalty of your own vicious scheme! Have him hanged immediately!" the king ordered, and the scheming Marcus received the end he so richly deserved. As for the Jews, the king declared publicly that he had every confidence in their loyalty. As a sign of his goodwill towards them, he ordered that they be freed from paying taxes for the next three years. When the Jews learned the full story of their narrow escape, their relief and joy can better be imagined than described. They all humbly thanked God for His benevolence towards them and resolved to serve Him with greater devotion in the future. They also decided to observe the 17th and 18th days of Shevat as days of prayer and joyous thanks to the Almighty, so that their children and future generations would remember the story of how they had been miraculously saved from destruction at the hands of a cruel enemy.

Switzerland

The Eternal Jew on the Matterhorn (see Wandering Jew)

> Mount Matter beneath the Matterhorn in Valais is a high glacier from which the Vispa River flows. According to popular legend, an imposing city existed there ages ago. The Jew came there once and said: "When I pass this way a second time there will be nothing but trees and rocks where you now see houses and streets. And when my path leads me here a third time, there will be nothing but snow and ice." And now nothing can be seen there but snow and ice.

Turkey

Folklore tells that some people are born with the power of the Evil Eye (al-ayn, Arabic) to cast a curse or a spell. At times, Jews were considered by tradition to be malevolent in that they deliberately cast the Evil Eye on their victims. The Evil Eye has its basis on the idea that the envious "nazar" (evil) glance of any passerby, attracted by an immodest show of wealth, achievement, or beauty, can harm or bewitch the unprotected person. Universally it is blamed for causing everything from bad luck and toothaches, to disease and death.

Newall (1973) suggests the Evil Eye to be part of the medieval concept of Jew as witch and cites witches Sabbath, witches' synagogue and that all enemies of society had the Evil Eye. The myth of the Evil Eye has developed into customs about how not to look at children, and in some cases, customs regarding not touching babies and restricting praise. Stating a child's name or age is thought to bring about the cursed eye, as well as whistling in a house, which is thought to invite it. In some families because of the fear of possible miscarriage from exposure to the evil eye, presents are never bought to an expectant mother until after the baby is born. The traditional admonishment "it's not polite to stare," could very well have stemmed from this fear of the eye. In modern Turkey as well as in the past, many parents keep new babies covered up in blankets for fear that their defenseless beauty will inspire a jealous glance. Its not uncommon in the Mediterranean countries for one wanting to speak of a child to say "oh, the child is so pretty—too bad he's dirty." "Mashallah," the customary Arabic greeting to the young translates into "may God preserve you from the evil eye."

One of the more creative political myths in Turkey was that the Young Turks' revolution was inspired by a Jewish-Freemason-Zionist conspiracy to take over the Ottoman Empire. The myth was eagerly adopted by Turkish opposition parties and Arab nationalists who used it to undermine the regime (Oke, 1986).

A very long time ago there was a woman who had a son. Both together one evening, the mother said to her son: "Go, my child, and shut the door, for I have fear." "What is fear?" the boy asked his mother. "When one is afraid," was the answer. "What then can this thing fear be?" pondered the son: "I will go and find it." So he set out, and came to a mountain where he saw forty robbers who lighted a fire and then seated them selves around it. The youth went up and greeted them, whereon one of the robbers addressed him:

"No bird dares to fly here, no caravan passes this place: how then dost thou dare to venture?"

"I am seeking fear; show it to me."

"Fear is here, where we are," said the robber.

"Where?" inquired the youth.

Then the robber commanded: "Take this kettle, this flour, fat, and sugar; go into that cemetery yonder and make helwa therewith."

"It is well," replied the youth, and went.

In the cemetery he lit a fire and began to make the helwa. As he was doing so a hand reached out of the grave, and a voice said: "Do I get nothing?" Striking the hand with the spoon, he answered mockingly: "Naturally I should feed the dead before the living." The hand vanished, and having finished cooking the helwa the youth went back to the robbers.

"Hast found it?" they asked him.

"No," replied he. "All I saw was a hand which appeared and demanded helwa; but I struck it with the spoon and saw no more of it."

The robbers were astonished. Then another of them remarked: "Not far from here is a lonely building; there you can, no doubt, find fear."

He went to the house, and entering, saw on a raised plat. form a swing in which was a child weeping; in the room a girl was running hither and thither. The maiden approached him and said: "Let me get upon your shoulders; the child is crying and I must quieten it." He consented, and the girl mounted. While thus occupied with the child, she began gradually to press the youth's neck with her feet until he was in danger of strangulation. Presently, with a jerk that threw him down, the girl jumped from his shoulders and disappeared. As she went a bracelet fell from her arm to the floor.

Picking it up, the youth left the house. As he passed along the road, a Jew, seeing the bracelet, accosted him. "That is mine," he said.

"No, it is mine," was the rejoinder.

"Oh, no, it is my property," retorted the Jew.

"Then let us go to the Cadi," said the youth. "If he awards it to thee, it shall be thine; if, however, he awards it to me, it remains in my possession."

So accordingly they went, and the Cadi said: "The bracelet shall be his who proves his case." Neither, however, was able to do this, and finally the judge ordered that the bracelet should be impounded till one of the claimants should produce its fellow, when it would be given up to him. The Jew and the youth then parted.

On reaching the coast, the boy saw a ship tossing to and fro out at sea, and heard fearful cries proceeding from it. He called out from the shore: "Have you found fear?" and was answered with the cry, "Oh, woe, we are sinking!" Quickly divesting him self of his clothes, he sprang into the water and swam toward the vessel. Those on board said: "Someone is casting our ship to and fro, we are afraid." The youth, binding a rope round his body, dived to the bottom of the sea. There he discovered that the Daughter of the Sea (Deniz Kyzy) was shaking the vessel. He fell upon her, flogged her soundly, and drove her away. Then, appearing at the surface, he asked: "Is this fear?" Without awaiting an answer he swam back to the shore, dressed himself, and went his way.

Now as he walked (along he saw a garden, in front of which was a fountain. He resolved to enter the garden and rest a little. Three pigeons disported themselves around the fountain. They dived down into the water, and as they came up again and shook themselves each was transformed into a maiden. They then laid a table, with drinking glasses. When the first carried a glass to her lips the others inquired: "To whose health drinkest thou?" She answered: "To that of the youth who, in making helwa, was not dismayed when a hand was stretched out to him from a grave." As the second maiden drank, the others again asked: "To whose health drinkest thou?" And the answer was: "To the youth on whose shoulders I stood, and who showed no fear though I nearly strangled him," Hereupon the third took up her glass. "Of whom art thou thinking?" questioned the others. "In the sea, as I tossed a ship to and fro," the maiden replied, "a youth came and flogged me so soundly that I nearly died. I drink his health."

Hardly had the speaker finished when the youth himself appeared and said: "I am that youth." All three maidens hastened to embrace him, and he proceeded: "At the Cadi's I have a bracelet that fell from the arm of one of you. A Jew would have deprived me of it but I refused to give it up. I am now seeking its fellow."

The maidens took him to a cave where a number of stately halls that opened before him overwhelmed him with astonishment. Each was filled with gold and costly objects. The maidens here gave him the second bracelet, with which he went directly to the Cadi and received the first, returning without loss of time to the cave. "You part from us no more," said the maidens. "That would be very nice," replied the youth, "but until I have found fear I can have no rest" Saying this he tore himself away, though they begged him earnestly to remain.

Presently he arrived at a spot where there was an immense crowd of people. "What is the matter?" the youth inquired, and was informed that the Shah of the country was no more. A pigeon was to be set free, and he on whose head the bird should alight would be declared heir to the throne. The youth stood among the curious sightseers. The pigeon was loosed, wheeled about in the air, and eventually descended on the youth's head. He was at once hailed as Shah; but as he was unwilling to accept the dignity a second pigeon was sent up. This also rested on the youth's head. The same thing happened a third time. "Thou art our Shah!" shouted the people. "But I am seeking fear; I will not be your Shah," replied he, resisting the efforts of the crowd to carry him off to the palace. His words were repeated to the widow of the late ruler, who said: "Let him accept the dignity for tonight at least; tomorrow I will show him fear." The youth consented, though he received the not very comforting intelligence that whoever was Shah one day was on the following morning a corpse. Passing through the palace, he came to a room in which he observed that his coffin was being made and water heated. Nevertheless, he lay down calmly to sleep in this chamber; but when the slaves departed he arose, took up the coffin, set it against the wall, lit a fire round it and reduced it to ashes. This done, he lay down again and slept soundly.

When morning broke, slaves entered to carry away the new Shah's corpse; but they rejoiced at beholding him in perfect health, and hurried to the Sultana with the glad tidings. She thereupon called the cook and commanded: "When you lay the supper tonight, put a live sparrow in the soup-dish."

Evening came. The young Shah and the Sultana sat down to supper, and as the dish was brought in the Sultana said: "Lift the lid of the dish." "No," answered the youth; "I do not wish for soup." "But please lift it," repeated the Sultana persuasively. Now as the youth stretched out his hand and lifted the lid, a bird flew out. The incident was so unexpected that it gave him a momentary shock of fear. "Seest thou! " cried the Sultana. "That is fear."

"Is it so?" asked the youth. "Thou wast indeed afraid," replied the Sultana.

Then the marriage feast was ordered, and it lasted forty days and forty nights. The young Shah had his mother brought to his palace and they lived happily ever after.

United States/Canada

There are no antisemitic folk tales in the United States or Canada. Yet the association of Jews with crucifixion and conspiracy to undermine Christendom transferred quietly from Europe. Researchers Rockaway & Gutfeld (2001) note that during the Nineteenth Century, depictions of Jews could be heard in sermons, and found in secular literature, specifically school texts and in the press. While demonic portrayals of Jews did not lead to the kinds of murderous outrages, pogroms or legal restrictions on Jews that characterized the European Jewish experience, such imagery remained a constant force in Nineteenth-Century America at times giving way to charges of Jewish treachery, sedition, radicalism, and conspiracy.

Louise Mayo (1988) reports that Jews were seen as the murderers of Christ, but hostile religious images diminished considerably by the end of the century. Literary caricatures and the press depicted the Jews as pawnbrokers and peddlers, with an overwhelming concern for wealth. Jews were also depicted as industrious, honorable, law-abiding, family-centered, and intelligent.

Public school and the Sunday schools frequently shared the same pupils and instilled similar Christian values. Jews were not viewed as a danger to the nation, but schoolbooks throughout America employed stereotypical negative depictions of Jews to emphasize their otherness. In local deliberations over abolishing test oaths for political office, at times politicians raised the deicide charge as one of the reasons for denying full political rights to Jews. In addition to reciting Protestant homilies, textbooks portrayed Jews as, among other things, unethical, greedy, disobedient, and wicked. The books also included the biblical accusations against Jews: children learned that the "Jews were the bitter enemies of the early Christians," that they had rejected and killed their savior, and that they were underlings of Satan. The deicide allegation surfaced in 1819 Maryland during regarding a bill granting Jews full citizenship, the so-called "Jew bill."

Rockaway & Gutfeld also cite key school texts *A Geography for Children* (1831) the *McGuffy Reader* and the *Encyclopaedia of English Grammar* (1849) that portrayed Jews as slayers and betrayers of Christ. School geographies insinuated that the Jews were a powerful people who controlled financial institutions and governments in Europe. A negative portrayal of a Jew made Harpers (1859) and at times newspapers ran stories of Jews as Christ-killers, Shylocks, and eternal aliens. In December of 1862, Ulysses S. Grant via Order #11 called for the expulsion of Jews "within twenty-four hours without trial or hearing" in Mississippi, Kentucky and Tennessee. But due to numerous protests from Jews and non-Jews, President Lincoln revoked the order.

Epilogue

◆

The Future of the Imaginary Jew

"Maybe they'll even stick us in ovens like Hansel and Gretel?"
  —Jews anticipating their fate during Nazi house arrest,
  from Von Trotta's 2003 film *Rosenstrasse.*

The future of the imaginary Jew is good. By contrast, real Jews are not fairing as well. With the sole exception of the United States, post 9/11 anti-Semitism rates and hate crimes against Jews have doubled in most nations where Jews reside. For the first time in Jewish history, the radical Right has joined forces with the extremist Arabic groups and the radical Left, anti-globalization forces, and liberal NGOs. Much of the increase is due to a steady stream of anti-Israeli rhetoric that has permeated the media over Palestinians so that the folkloric Jews are linked to real Jews. Some of it is misinformation, some of it is to jump on a liberal bandwagon, and some of it is just plain antisemitism as correlation studies have shown (Baum and Nakazawa 2007). The geography and citizenship does not seem to matter. "I am angry at Israel," said Naveed Haq, age 30, when he explained why he wounded five and killed one worker at a Seattle Jewish Center.

It is always the case that when the imaginary Jew is believed in, real Jews' lives are in jeopardy. Social myths are vital to understanding anti-semitc beliefs. In 1993, Bryn Mawr political scientist Marc Howard Ross analyzed ninety cultures and the factors that caused conflict within them and concluded that myths were the literal smoking gun of group conflict. The psycho-cultural factors were "assumptions, perceptions and images about the world that are widely shared with others and not idiosyncratic" (Ross 1993, 10). Sociologist Helen Fein reached similar conclusions in 1979 when she observed a statistical correlation between popular anti-Semitism and the number of Jews killed during the Holocaust. One does not need statistics as much as history to know that myth is the handmaiden of antisemitism.

The problem is not one of history, but one of psychology.[1] It is all too easy to shift national narratives and sway public opinion. The word "Jew" conveys ambiguity and importance, which are key ingredients for rumor transmission. The processes that keep rumors, superstitions, and urban legends alive also propel antisemitc myths. Charismatic leaders help, but they are not always necessary, as the leaderless Danish cartoon riots of 2006 attest. Much more important is a simple, appealing tale that is concise, consistent with what people already know, and just crazy enough to threaten and unnerve them.

Historian Ian Kershaw almost got it right: the road to Auschwitz was indeed built by hate. But it wasn't "paved with indifference" so much as fantasy, lore, and antisemitc myth.

"What good fortune for those in power that the people do not think," Hitler once said. He and Goebbels, and all propagandists, understood that people are prone to certain fantasies and do not want too much reality. There is right and wrong, and good and bad. In lieu of more complicated understanding, they watch and wait for the next undermining act of the Jews.

The Jews they are waiting for are not real people but are superstitions, folklores, and fantasies. With precedent from history and church and state support, who would ever doubt the malevolence of the Jews as those who would undermine all that is good, godly and right? Whether it is true does not seem to matter. Jews must be contained. Jews must not be trusted. Never has there been a better villain. "If the Jew did not exist, we would have to invent him," Sartre once said.

Folkloric Jews are on our mind, while real Jews roam the planet. As long as people are unable to separate fantasy from reality, the real Jews fate remains precarious – contingent on, of all things, a fairy tale.

◆   ◆   ◆

Postscript

In a compilation of antisemitc myths, it seems fitting to balance Jewish legends that depict the rich folk life of medieval Jewry. The reader is referred to the works of Sholem Aleichem (1859–1916) and the early Yiddish or Polish literature depicting village life.

Many of the surviving legends have themes of social acceptance and survival. Jews who have made it to the top of the Roman Catholic hierarchy e.g. *The Jewish Pope*. Other tales involve intervention from God, such as *The Rashi Wall*. This tale occurs in Worms, Germany, where in 1624, the wall at the Rashi Chapel was said to have moved backward in order to save the life of a poor woman who was in danger of being crushed by a passing cart in the narrow street.

But the most famous legend originating from medieval Europe was that of the Golem.

> According to the Sixteenth Century lore, Rabbi Loew built a Golem to defend Prague's Jews from anti-Semitic attacks. A Golem was a Frankenstein like creature which could only be made from the clay of the Vltava River. Following the prescribed rituals, the rabbi made him come to life by reciting special incantations in Hebrew. As the Golem grew bigger, he also became more violent and started killing people and spreading fear. Violence against the Jews would stop if the Golem was destroyed. The Rabbi agreed. To destroy the Golem, he rubbed out the first letter of the word "emet" from the golem's forehead to make the Hebrew word "met." meaning death. According to legend, the Golem of Prague's remains are stored in a coffin in the attic of the Altneuschul in Prague, and it can be summoned again if needed.

APPENDIX

Limericks, Proverbs, Poems Pilgrimages and Shrines, Media and Popular Support, Hate Group Folk Beliefs, Legalized Folk Beliefs, A Millennium of Antisemitc Beliefs

A Jew clipping money

LIMMERICKS, PROVERBS, POEMS

Child of torture, son of shame, robbed of even a father's name—
In this year of Christian grace, What's your state of what's your place?
Why you're rich and strong and gave Chakey Eisnstein ouff Broadway.
Fat and rich you are and loud, fond of being in a crowd ...
Fond of life and fond of fun, (Once your beezness wholly done)
Openhanded generous free, full of Christian charity:
far more full than him who pikes at your avarice his jokes.
Fond of friends and ever kind to the sick and lame and blind;
(And though loud you else may be—Silent in your charity)
Fond of Mrs. Einstein and her too numerous infant band.
Ever willing they should share your enjoyment everywhere ...
Though you're spurned in some hotels, you have kin among the swells—
Great musicians, poets true, painters, singers not a few
Owe their cousinship to you ... Well good friend we look at you and behold the
conquering Jew.
—from the British periodical Puck (1891).

And the Jew with crooked heel
Crooked nose and crooked pants
Slithering towards the stock exchange
Deeply corrupted and without soul.
—Wilhelm Busch

The Jew is a poor wretch!
His own women don't appeal to him!
He thinks he's terribly clever
When he steals a German woman
The father says to the daughter:
'A dreadful worry plagues me!
We are all of pure blood!
You however, out of interest,
For the sake of fine clothes and money
Are seeing the Jew Sali Rosenfeld
And even talk about becoming his wife!
It's not on, no way, listen well:
One would never hitch a dachshund
In a yoke intended for a cow!
It's just not possible!

Ballad of The Cruel Jews Wife (Ireland,1826, abridged)

She came to the Jew's wife's house
Tapping at the window
Saying little Hugh if you be here
O let your Mamma in
No says the Jew's wife then
He was not here today
He went out with the little boys
To have some pretty play

… She rolled me in a leaden sheet
Which weigh full many a pound.
And threw me down in the Dam water
Which was so dark and cold.(Hultin, 1988)

Ballad of Little Sir Hugh (England, 1783)

She's led him in through ae dark door,
And sae has she thro' nine;
She's laid him on a dressing-table,
And stickit him like a swine.

And first came out the thick, thick blood,
And syne came out the thin;
And syne came out the bonny heart's blood;
There was nae mair within.

She's row'd him in a cake o'lead,
Bade him lie still and sleep;
She's thrown him in Our Lady's draw-well
Was fifty fathom deep.

Short the pants and long the jacket Crooked the nose as is the cane
Eyes black and gery the soul Hat to the rear, shrewd the mien,
Such is Sammy Crookedlegs

Behold I am the rootless one Not wedded to the world I see
No homesick daydreams frightens me For I am steeled by suffering
Go on and drive me from your portals Still I am the one most longed for'
Your sheiks of envy pierce the air For I weigh your values and you decide
The slippery membranes of my soul Conceal what beggin I once yielded
And still my plunder rises high And your women pay me tribute
Me the outcast of alien deserts Yawning you smoke your tobacco
For your esteemed digestions sake But I I probe with crafty fingers
And I provoke your depravity For my own great delectation
And thus I play the little games Of my overripe high spirits
The strange subtle final ends Concealed from you of my Asiatic blood.

> Get a bit of pork
> Stick it on a fork'
> And give it to a Jew boy Jew.
> —18th Century British children's rhyme

Proverbs

The Jews are the Devil's Christians (German)
If the Jew is baptized, the devil stands as the godfather.(Swabian/German)
So long as there are Jews, the world is full of the devil, (Austrian)
Jews and grocers are friends with the Devil (German)
He thought he caught a Jew by the beard but he held the Devil by the horns (Polish)
Where there are Jews and embers, bring the Devil (German)
Where the Devil cannot act, the Jew can (Polish)
The Jew is the Devil's drill (Hungarian)
Devils skin (name of cloth used for Jewish caftan (Romanian)
Devil dances on the wall with his Jewess by the scruff (Romanian)
Go to the Jews/Go to the Devil (curse) (Romanian)
One two three times To hell with the Kikes (called out at dances) (Romanian)
Out pops the devil from under the grass, The Jew leads his by his locks/pais (Romanian)
If the Jew knew that the sow had swallowed a half Kpec, he would eat it.(Ukraine)
The Jew and the devil sleep in one bed (Swabian/German)
The Jew and Jew money destroy the world(German)

Recited in chorus:

From a Jew's countenance-the evil devil talks to us,
The devil, who in every land-is known as evil plague.
If we shall be free of the Jew-and again will be happy and glad,
Then the youth must struggle with us-to subdue the Jew devil.
—Instructor's manual, The Poison Mushroom

Michigan State University Football Chant
(Sung to the University of Michigan theme as a taunt)
Hail to the book of Moses
Hail to their crooked noses
Hail, Hail to Michigan
The Israel of the West.

Throw the Jew down the well.
So my country can be free.
You must grab him by his horns.
Then we'll have a big party!
—from the film Borat, (2006) www.youtube.com/watch?v=Vb3IMTJjzfo

Mini-Antisemitic Legends

—In Lancashire County England, a golden plover (bird) is said to embody the Wandering Jew and calls all night.

—The Seven Whistlers (birds) are said to be souls of Jews who crucified Christ and foretell of death and disaster.

—Cornish tin mines are haunted by *the knockers* (Jews) so blocks of tin found in bogs are called Jews Tin. (The White Thursday—the week before Christmas day—was claimed by tinners as a holiday (Jew-whidn), because on this day, black tin (tin ore) was first melted and refined into white tin. Today Jew-whidn is a name given to the old furnaces and old smelting houses are called Jews'-houses.

—For those gravely ill, a Rabbi prays for recovery to hasten death.(Germany)

—To ward off evil one must spit after uttering the word Jew. (Spain)

—It is unlucky to meet a Jew first thing in the morning. (Germany)

—It is unlucky to have a Jew look through your window or enter your house on a Monday. Unluckiness lasts all week. (Eastern Europe) (See Poland and Romania).

Montefiore
Londres

Heraldry

Jews in the Middle Ages used heraldic emblems. One example is found in early 14th century Narbonne (France), where Kalonymos bar Todros, nasi or head of the Jewish community, used a lion rampant. The seal of Benoît, Jew of Dôle (France), was placed on a loan document at the request of the borrowing knight in 1286 (the seal shows a lion contourné). A manuscript of 1383 shows the arms of Samuel, son of Doctor Samuel of Venice, per fess a lion issuant and a fess wavy. A number of Jewish or converted Jewish families used three Jews' hats on their arms, either arranged two and one or in pair conjoined by their straps. One amusing example is the seal of Byfegin, from Koblenz (1397) which bears a lion rampant "crowned" with a Jew's hat. Nostradamus, the famous 16th c. astrologer who settled in France, bore: Gules, a wheel broken between each spoke or. Since the color of the charge was too clear a reminder of the bearer's origins, a descendant had the arms changed to quarterly, 1 and 4 Argent a wheel sable; 2 and 3 Argent an eagle's head erased sable. Several seals were those of the Jewish community of a city: early 13th century examples in France show that the Jews of Paris used an eagle rising on a semis of fleurs-de-lis. Jewish communities also had flags which they used in processions; the synagogue in Prague has a 16th c. example, showing a Jew's hat within a star of David. Several Hungarian Jews were mint masters in the 13th centuries and issued coins on behalf of the king with their Hebrew initial letter on the reverse. Some of them are also known in official documents as "counts of the treasury", and seem to have formed part of the Hungarian nobility. They disappeared in the last quarter of the 13th century. http://www.heraldica.org/topics/jewish.htm

CHRISTIAN PILGRIMAGE TO HONOR THE BLOOD LIBEL

Andrel, martyred by 'The Jews'

—Anderl von Rinn (Austria) (d. 1462) literally "they cut throat of the martyr and take all blood from him." A cultus of Anderl von Rinn began in 1621 the body was transferred to the churchyard of Judenstein (JewStone) in 1985. The cult was officially forbidden in 1994 though some make a procession to his grave every year. [Feast Day July 12].

Bury St. Edmunds (England) (d. 1181) Robert a Christian child was murdered by The Jews (Benedictine Shrines at Norwich, Gloucester, Bury, Lincoln). The Bury or Cloisters' Cross, a 12 Century ivory relic depicting the Jews as killers of Christ is displayed at St. Edmundsbury Cathedral, Suffolk UK.

—Conrad of Weissensee (Germany) d. 1303

—Deggendorf (Germany) (1338) Host Desecration festival honored until 1992, when the bishop Muller of Regensburg extinguished it and erected a plaque correcting this falsified history. Some still honor the site.

—Dominic of Val/San Domenichino de Val (Spain) d 1250 Altar boy Saragossa. The St. Nicolas Church alter reads "Murdered by Jews in 1250". His body glowed in Seo Cathedral a brightly lit chapel for pilgram visits. [Feast Day August 31] The Little Dominic feast is celebrated throughout Aragon, Spain.

—Herbert of Huntingdon (England), d. 1180

—Hugh of Lincoln (England) (d, 1255) A well was constructed in Jews' Court neighborhood advertised as the well in which Hugh's body was found. In 1955, the Anglican Church replaced the shrine at Lincoln Cathedral with an apologia. Feast day: July 27

—Joanniken von Siegburg (Germany) d 1287

—Louis or Ludwig of Ravensburg (Germany) d. 1429 Easter. [Feast Day April 30].

—Lorenzino Sossio (Italy) d. 1485 age 5, killed on Good Friday. [Feast Day.April 15

—Niño de La Guardia (Spain) d. 1491 "Little Nino" is believed to have been martyred by The Jews of La Guardia Spain. No body had been found, because it had been taken directly up to heaven. The blind mother of Nino was said to have had her sight miraculously restored at the moment that the child died. A 1992, Israeli Television series entitled "Out of Spain 1492" conducted local interviews. Several La Guardia residents interviewed for Israeli TV claimed that the story was true or could have been true. The town celebrates an annual pageant honoring Santo Niño and a commemorative statue has been erected in the town plaza. http://www.cryptojews.com/Santo_Nino.htm (see Blood Libel)

—Richard of Pontoise(France) d. 1179

—Robert (see Bury St. Emunds)

—Rudolf of Berne(Switzerland), d. 1294

—Simon of Trent (Italy) d.1475 Patron Saint of antisemitism. The cultus/beatification occurred in 1588 by Pope Sixtus but was invalidated by Pope Paul in 1965. In 2001 the local authorities of the Autonomous Province of Trento promoted a common Catholic and Jewish prayer at the site.

—Werner of Oberwesel (Germany), d. 1287. Employed by Jews and received Communion then they killed him. [Feast Day. April 19]

—William of Norwich (England) d. 1144 (see Blood Libel)

—Vièrge de Valreas (France) d. 1247

ANTISEMITIC SHRINES AND FESTIVALS

Judensau, St. Mary's Church, Wittenberg, Germany (2007)

—Arma Christi (England) display depicts The Jews spitting at Christ.

—Bertesgarten Germany. Annual visitation of 150,000 highlighted on Hitler's birthday.

—Brussels Belgium St. Michael-St. Gudle Cathedral Stained glass and tapestry of antisemitic folklore.

—Deggendorf, Germany. Holy Sepulchre Church. Bleeding Host, believed to be intact from 1137 to 1900. Display of tin plaque over crucifiction relief of 'godless Jews' removed in 1968. Host art has been removed from Iphofen and morphored into a spiderweb grate since 1984. The Bishop of Regensburge discontinued the pilgrimage in 1992, though some still unofficially continue.

—Judenberg, Austria. A curious stone on the southwest corner of a large brick Gothic church in Sternberg Germany. Mortared into the wall of a chapel that juts out beside what was once the main portal of the church, the stone bears, deeply embedded in it, large prints of two bare feet, on the edges of which chisel marks are visible. The stone, which was incorporated into the wall in 1496, is one on which the wife of the Jew Eleazar is said to have stood when she tried to sink a desecrated Host in the nearby creek. Unable to cast away the host, she supposedly

sank into the stone, Sixty-five Jews were tortured and confessed to the Host desecration. Twenty-seven were executed by burning. (Bynum, 2004)

—Judensau (Jew Pig)
Currently displayed in Aarschot, Belgium (Notre Dame Church); Bamberg
(Cathedral); Basel, Switzerland (Cathedral); Brandenburg (Cathedral); Bayreuth
(town church); Cadolzburg; Va;be (Stephanie Chuch); Colmarer (St Martin
Cathedral) ; Cologne (Chorgestuehl in the Cathedral and St. Severin); Eber-
swalde (Maria Magdalena); Erfurt (Cathedral); Frankfurt; Freising; Gnesner;
Holy City; Heilsbronner;; Lemgoer; Magdeburger(Cathedral); Metz, France;
Nuremberg (St Sebaldus Church); Regensburg; Remagen (Gate elbow);Theilen-
berg; Uppsala, Sweden (Cathedral); Wiener Neustadt, Austria; Wimpfen
(Church of St. Peter); Wittenberg (Town Church) Xantener ; Zerbst (St Nicolas
Church).

—Judenstein, Austria, Ceiling fresco in the church commemorating Andrew of
Rinn murder-pilgrimmage. When city of Linz Jews protested, bishop Rusch
responded with "The Jews have not up to the present time ever proved that they
never commited a parallel crime [of ritual murder]" Dundes, 1991 p.343) By
1961, Pope John XXIII had a plague installed stating that the case of Andrew of
Rinn was a legend that had "nothing to do with the Jewish people." and sup-
pressed the cult of Andrew. The village became defiant and left the statue intact.
Related Jewish towns of Judenbuchel, and Judengrube.

—Heiligengrabe Germany. Host desecration painting

—Korneuberg Austria, Church santuary

—La Alberca Spain, Festival. A pig "El Marrano" (converted Jew) is released to
run through the village.

—Leon Province Spain. During Easter, cafeterias offer special lemonade in bot-
tles that "will be used to kill Jews." see J.L. Gonzales Arpide (1999) A Fuego
Lento, Leon, 1 April.

—Marina di Masia, Italy A blood libel poetry contest

—Ootmarsum, Overijssel province (Holland). On Easter, young men chant of Jews culpable for Jesus's death as they walk in a procession through their village. The OJEC has asked the Archbishop of Utrecht to publicly denounce the singing of these songs. The provisional answers from the Board of the diocese is variegated but negative.

—Passau, Germany. Holy Savior Church Bleeding Host pilgrimage

—Pulkau, Austria. Alterpiece commemorating Man of Sorrows, called by some as the patron of pogroms. Host desecration allegations triggered the massacre of Pulkau's Jewish community of 150 on April 23, 1338 via drowning, burning, decapition and evisceration. "The mythical Jew posed an existential peril to the empire—a peril from which the altar's celestial patron offered protection and deliverance," notes historian Mitchell Merback (2005). The wings depicting the Host desecration are currently not on dislay and Nurembuerg's museum painting of the Regensburg Host is not either but the Nicolas Brue altar is available.

—Poland/Eastern Europe Alina Cala (1995) cites folk festivals where ceremonial Jews are displayed or people join the procession wearing Jew masks and clothing. The Corpus Christi Church in Poznan Poland has a crypt of the well where Jews threw a desecrated Host. At the Feast of Booths, Jews are celebrated as rainmakers.

—Regensburg Germany. Fed up by economic competition and a 1476 blood Libel, popular uprisings in 1493 and 1513 brought new levels of anti-Jewish politics. In 1519, the citizens of Regensburg had expelled the Jews and were celebrating the expulsion by demolishing the synagogue. During the demolition, stonemason Jacob Kern was seriously injured and was taken to his home to receive last rites. Kern's wife meanwhile prayed to the Virgin Mary to spare her husband's life. Miraculously Kern recovered and returned to work. He said that throughout the ordeal the Virgin Mary had held him in her hand. Anti-Jewish violence increased as a result and within a month a wooden chapel was erected on the ruins of the synagogue to receive a flood of pilgrims seeking aid of the Virgin of Regensburg. Several Marian sitings were noted. (Creasman, 2002)

—Segovia Spain, festival commemorating the confiscated synagogue (its leaders executed) after the earthquake of 1415 was interpreted as a divine retaliation for Jewish blood rituals.

—Urbino, Italy. Paintings by Paolo Uccello on the predella for the altarpiece of the Communion of the Apostles in the Ducal Palace. In one scene, a Jewish family stands transfixed as a Christian mob batters down the door to their house, alerted to a host desecration by the miraculous flow of blood through the walls of the house. One of the two Jewish children weeps in terror, while a younger sibling clings to the mother 's skirts. A subsequent panel shows the same family, bound together at the stake, as the flames consume them.

SOUVENIRS & GIFTS

Turn of the 19th Century German beer stein which states "Hail to the Kosher Nation." On one side and "Raus! Raus Deutschland." (Out, out of Germany on the other). Includes scene of a Jewish bank.

MICELLANEOUS

From the 1950s to the mid-1980's Mary Ann Van Hoof (1909–1984) received antisemitic "visions" from the Virgin Mary telling her that the Rothschild's are "mongrel Yids" bent on world domination and from poverty to world wars, the Jews and their "satanic secret society" were involved. Located in La Crosse Wisconsin the Necedah Shrine is open to the public but not recognized by the Catholic Church.

Passion Plays are theater representing the trial and death have been traditionally performed during Lent. These plays depict a crowd of Jews condemning Jesus death and a Jewish leader assuming guilt. Violence against Jews often occurred. According to James Shapiro, author of *Oberammergau* (Vintage, 2001), the play has been performed every decade since 1634. Hitler praised the 1930s production and when it was performed in the year 2000, the language that at times incited crowds to torch nearby Jewish communities had been modified.

Happy Easter!

A disproportionate number of antisemitic hate crimes are committed during Easter as many Christian churches implicate The Jews in the death of Jesus. The following news stories were noted in April 2001.

—Conservative Christian leader and head of the Free Congress Foundation, Paul Weyrich writes that "Christ was crucified by the Jews." (April 24, 2001)

—NBA point guard Charlie Ward said in an interview that Jews were persecuting Christians and "had his [Jesus'] blood on their hands." "There are Christians getting persecuted by Jews every day. There's been books written about this—people who are raised Jewish and find Christ, then their parents stop talking to them." Concluding the Bible-study, power forward Kurt Thomas offered Konigsberg, who is Jewish, "[Y]ou know, there's Jews for Jesus, man.(April 22, 2001)

—"B.C." comic depicted a menorah disintegrating into a cross, with each panel reciting Jesus's last words: "Father, forgive them, for they know not what they do." (April, 22, 2001)

MEDIA/POPULAR CULTURE

Friday 30. Jun 2006

The Guardian has removed obscene antisemitic messages from its website following a protest by Board of Deputies Public Affairs Director Fiona Macaulay. The messages were posted under pseudonyms on a Talk Board on the 'Guardian Unlimited' site and alleged that Jews use Palestinian blood to make Matzo: the unleavened bread eaten on Passover. Fiona Macaulay commented, "That the blood libel of mediaeval antisemitic folklore should be appearing on a 21st century British website is huge cause for concern. The individuals responsible for posting such obscenities on the internet are clearly virulent antisemites who are taking advantage of the current climate of anti-Israel feeling in Britain. To even attempt to dress this up as legitimate criticism of Israel is ridiculous and I am pleased that The Guardian has responded to our protests by removing the messages and banning those responsible from using the Talk Board in future. "Had they not done so we would have had no choice but to go to the Press Complaints Commission to file a complaint under anti-incitement legislation." The Board's action on this follows its condemnation of an article that appeared in a Saudi government newspaper which claimed to have 'discovered' that Jews use the blood of non-Jewish children to make pastries for the festival of Purim. Board Director General, Neville Nagler, has written to the Saudi Ambassador in London asking him to disown the allegations on behalf of the Saudi government.

(See Shindler, 2004)

http://www.bod.org.uk/bod/index.jsp?page=extra&address=press/press_artical.jsp&id=344

July 27, 1997
Belarusian state television broadcast a documentary about the life and death of
Saint Gavril Belostoksky. Throughout the program, it was insinuated that Jews
had killed the child to use his blood in the making of Passover matzoth. Though
this libelous charge has been discredited for almost a century, the people of
Belarus were told this false version of the story as a "historical truth."

Nov. 1998 Romania Mare Issue #437
In Romania, the strongest branch of a Masonic Satanic sect activates with men
infiltrated in each and every top structures of the state ... which keeps only Jews
in the most important positions.

Oct. 28, 2000 Al-Ahram Newspaper (Egypt)
"A Jewish matza made from Arab Blood" is serialized.

Al Ahram's government appointed editor of Ibrahim Nafie defended the decision
to print as history and charged that a pending court case in France "can be considered a form of ideological terrorism and a way to cripple freedom of the press
in Egypt and the Arab world."
"French Court, Egyptian Spar over antisemtic article." Boston Globe 8/2/02 p. A
25 For mulitple examples of Arab press antisemitism, see MEMRI.org

Certainly the Jew is the very devil incarnal.
—Merchant of Venice (II scene 2)

To the Jew becoming a man signifies above all, to discontinue being a Jew.
—Richard Wagner from Judaism in Music, 1850.

"Just one of the many imaging solutions you didn't expect to find from
Polaroid." Slogan from advertisement depicting three Hasidic Jews peering at a
cache of diamonds in a bank basement vault. (Ad ran in *Business Week*, June 6,
2000 p.7 and *Newsweek*)

Polaroid's response to ADL complaint.
As you may know, there have been numerous documentaries created about the
diamond vaults in New York, and in keeping with the spirit of documentaries,
we made every effort to maintain the integrity of the diamond industry in our
advertisement. As a result, we thought a diamond vault was a perfect scenario to

depict the Polaroid Fingerprint Security Reader, and do not believe that this ad degrades the diamond dealer community or the Jewish community in any way. www.adl.org/PresRele/Mise_00/3647_00.asp

F*****g Jews … The Jews are responsible for all the wars in the world. Are you a Jew?"—Mel Gibson actor, during DUI arrest, 2006

The descendants of such who crucified Christ, the descendants of such who threw to Bolivar from here and also crucified [them] in Santa Marta, back in Colombia. A minority has appropriated the wealth of the world, a minority has appropriated gold of the planet, the silver, minerals, waters, good land, petroleum—the wealth, then, and have concentrated the wealth in few hands.
—Hugo Chavez, Prime Minister of Venezuela, Christmas Speech, 2006

St. Thomas Augustus
"The Jew should not be allowed to keep what they've attained from others through usury. It would help that they earn their living instead of doing nothing."

T.S. Eliot
The rat is underneath the piles. The Jew is underneath the lot.

Pope Clement VIII
"All the world suffers from the usury of the Jews, their monopoly and deceit. They have brought many unfortunate people into a state of poverty. Especially the farmers, working class people, and the very poor."

Ulysses S. Grant
I have observed that despite all the vigilance that can be infused in our commanders, the special regulations of the treasury department have been violated, mostly by Jews. As such, I have refused all permits allowing Jews to come South. I have had them frequently expelled from the department, but they come with their carpet sacks despite all that can be done to prevent it.

Napoleon Bonaparte
The Jews are the Master Robbers of the modern age. They must be treated with political justice, not with civil justice. They are surely not real citizens. They have practiced usury since the time of Moses, and oppressed other peoples. We should

ban Jews from commerce, because they abuse it. The Evils of the Jew do not stem from the individual, but from the fundamental nature of this people.

Jerome, King of Phalia
I seek to improve the Jews, but I do not want anymore of them in my kingdom. Indeed I have done all I can to improve my scorn of the most vile people in the world.

St Justin
The Jews were behind all the persecutions of the Christians. They wandered through the county hating and undermining the Christian faith.

Houston Stewart Chamberlain
The revelation of Christ has no significance for the Jew. I have searched through entire libraries of Jewish literature with the expectation to find not the divinity of Christ or the idea of redemption, but the purely human feeling for the greatness of a suffering savior, but in vain. A Jew who feels that is in fact no longer a Jew, but a denier of Judaism.

Martin Luther
The Sun never did shine on a more vengeful and blood-thirst people as they, who proclaim to be the people of God, who desire to and think they must murder and crush the heathen

What are we going to do with these rejected, condemned Jewish People? Let us apply the ordinary wisdom of nations like France, Spain, Bohemia, who made them give account of what they had stolen through usury. Divide it evenly, but expel them from the country"

Even with no further evidence than the old testament, I would maintain that no person on earth could alter my opinion that the Jews as they are today are veritably a mixture of all the depraved and benevolent naves the whole world over.

Cicero
The Jews belong to a dark and repulsive force. One knows the power they exercise through their unions. They are a nation of rascals and deceivers.

Richard Wagner
The Jew has never had an art of his own; hence, never alive of art enabling import. So long as the separate art of music have a real organic need in it, down to the epochs of Mozart and Beethoven, there was no where to be found a Jewish composer. It was quite impossible for an element foreign to that living organism to take a part in the formative stages in that life.

Kaiser Wilhem II
A Jew cannot be a true patriot. He is something different, like a bad insect. He must be kept apart, out of a place where he can do mischief

Cardinal Mindszenty
The trouble makers in Hungary are the Jews. They demoralize our country

George Bernard Shaw
This is the real enemy. The invader from the East. The ruffian, the oriental parasite. In a word, the Jew.

Voltaire
Why are the Jews hated? It is the inevitable result of their laws. They either must conquer everyone, or be hated by the whole of Humanity.

H.G. Wells
The Jews looked for a special savior; a messiah who was to redeem mankind by the agreeable process of restoring the glories of David, and bringing the world at last under the firm but benevolent Jewish Heel.

Zionism is an expression of Jewish refusal to assimilate. If the Jews have suffered, it is because they've regarded themselves as a chosen people

Jews do not adequately realized the irritations they inflict

Ralph Waldo Emerson
The sufferance which is the badge of the Jew, has made him in these days the ruler of the rulers of the Earth.

Henry Wallace
Truman was exasperated over Jewish pressure that he support Zionist rule over Palestine. He expressed himself as being very much put-out with the Jews.

President Truman
Christ couldn't please them [the Jews] when he was on the Earth, so how could anyone expect that I would have any luck? I have no use for them, and couldn't care what happens to them

---

For further reading see Allan Gould's What did they think of Jews? (Jason Aronson, 1991)

ANTISEMTIC MYTHS AS POLITICAL IDEOLOGY

The Black Hebrew Israelites (BHI) believe that Blacks represent Gods true 'chosen people' while condemning Whites as evil. As the authentic Jews, BHI deems Jews as impostors. BHI adherents wear black clothing with emblems of the Star of David. Chicago's Ben Ami Ben Israel (nee:Ben Carter) heard "a voice tell me that the time had come for Africans in America the decedents of the Biblical Israelites to return to the land of our forefathers" and accompanied a group to settle in Israel that since 1967. Other groups are popularized by Yahweh Ben Yahweh (nee Hulon Mitchell Jr), Louis Farrakhan and Leonard Jeffries who hold part or whole of the following tenets: Whites are cold, materialistic, evil ice people residing in Europe's colder climates. Blacks are sun people originating in Africa. They are "warm, humanistic and sensitive." The English are elephants, Dutch are squirrels and Jews as skunks. Other beliefs implicate the U.S. military and Jewish doctors to have created AIDS, Jews as leaders in the slave trade and that the statue of Liberty has chains at the bottom representing slavery. Specifically, NOI's beliefs focus on Wallace Fard a Detroit door-to-door salesman claimed his birth in Mecca and sold a belief that God was African and under 23 god-scientists the chosen people led by the tribe Shabazz raised the empires of Africa. Mr. Yacub an evil god-scientitst created experiments that produced the devilish White race and they were exiled to the island of Patmos but he continued his evil work to defeat Africans. The blue eyed devils were exiled again to the ice caves of Europe who were eventually civilized by Moses and Jesus as a favor to Allah. Six thousands years of the above scenes are thought to end in 1914 and the tribe of Shabazz will reclaim their original glory the real chosen ones replacing the 144,000 Jews in the Revelation.

British-Israelism: The Jews are impostures. The real Jews are the British as are those of general Celtic-Saxon heritage. Variations of this include the following: Two branches of humanity fashioned from one of the Twelve tribes of Israel; with the others the darker races God created on a different day. Early in history, Sephardic people came down from the north in the Middle East supplanted the original Jews and drove out the Chosen people and for centuries these quisling have conspired to rule the earth through the institutions of finance. The true Chosen of God were of the original Twelve tribes and are now the White race.

Militia: Another ideology seems to have evolved from the French Revolution when citizenship was granted to Jews. In this version, the French revolution resulted from the Order of Templars (secret Order to protect religious pilgrims en route to the Holy Land). While most were burned at the stake in 1314, some were thought to have escaped. The Templars plot against the Papacy and civil liberties and are believed to have infiltrated the Order of Freemasons (Liberal principled stone masons). The Illuminati (rationalistic philosophers) are also involved whose liberalism was spread to the Jews.

Another belief of the militia indicts The Federal Reserve as controlled by 8 unnamed Jewish families. Tax dollars are funding affirmative action and welfare at the expense of Whites and a New World Order will supplant the U.S. government with UN supported Hong Kong police flying black helicopters protecting this New World Order. Militia based conspiracies begin with a secret controlling economic and political elite. The elite can take the form of the Bilderbergers, Members of the Bilderberg together with their 'sister' organizations-the Trilateral Commission (known also as the "Child of Bilderberg") and the Council on Foreign Relations. The UN troops will lead a military coup in order to create a socialist One World Government run by Jews (Protocols of Zion based Zionist Organized Government—ZOG), Communists and the U.N. The following is believed to occur: 1) private property rights and gun ownership will be abolished 2) all national state and local elections will be controlled by the U.N. 3) the U.S. constitution will be supplanted by the U.N charter 4) only approved churches that will be under control of One World Religion 5) UNESCO will control all education.

Revelation/Christian End Times: End Times is a philosophy written in 95 AD, as the Revelation to St. John the Divine. The belief is that a series of catastrophic events culminates in the near success of the antichrist and the Messiah appears. The Messiah destroys the antichrist, redeems the chosen, establishes a new heaven on earth for the next thousand years. End Times tales have been updated in a series of best selling novels (40 million sold) by Tim LaHaye's Left Behind. In the End of Time, apocalyptic good triumphs over evil, a select 144,000 Jews are saved, false prophets and tests of faith occur. Good is defined as the faithful, meek, poor, socially deprived, politically disenfranchised, ill and outcast. Conversely, Evil is defined as everyone else. In the past evil/devil has included the monarchy, wealthy landlords, challenging clergy, those not born-again and the mythic Jew. Rev. Pat Robertson's version of End Times includes a secret sinister Jewish based society.

The militia's version of End Times focuses more on planetary takeover and enslavement. Indicted again are the 'cosmopolitan liberal secular Jews' the U.N.

the Masons, communists and capitalists. A New World Order is to be created run by liberal minded elite. The Order of Illumanati are involved as are the Knights Templar and an array of conspirators. For the patriot/militia, history was hijacked by sinister forces who killed the kings of France and Sweden and create party purges under both Lenin and Stalin. Moses Hess and the Rothchilds with the Illuminists and Freemasons are implicated in the menacing anti-American communism. Some versions include the Wilson administration's Federal Reserve Board, war profiting Jews, Zionists.

Armageddon evolves as a war with Jews (Devil) promoting the UN and New World Order. Aryans become the true Israel establishing Gods kingdom and are appointed to identify violations of God's laws—internationalism, Mark of the Beast (666) and race-mixing. Phineas Priests, a faction of Christian Identity, use Chapter 25 of the Book of Numbers to justify killing those who race mix. Their belief is that God granted everlasting priesthood to Phineas for killing an Israelite having sex with a Midianite.

Aryans and UFOs: Odinism is a neo-pagan pre-Christian mythology similar to Asatru (Iceland) that includes Odin the warlike father of all other gods; Frey, his clairvoyant wife; Thor, his hammer wielding son and multiple others. The ideas here are based on the martyrdom of a Teutonic warrior who finds glory in death as he crosses over to Valhalla (Hall of the Slain—part of Odin's special army) on a blazing funeral pyre. The volkisch writings of philosopher and biblical ideologues as Eugen Dubrind and Paul de Lagarde and composer Richard Wagner blended neoromanticism, nationalism, Christianity, Aryanism and the the Bayreuth circle spirit as the mainstay of Wagnerian antisemitism. Wagner later established an intellectual community at Bayreuth that romanticized German history and myths ie., Siegfried, the ideal Aryan blond and moral warrior.

All hate groups hold a vision of racial utopia. Many combine Nordic gods, black magic, occultism and devil worship with Nazi philosophy. Indian writer Savitri Devi who linked the swastika of Eastern mysticism to the 'spiritual avatar' Hitler, Italian Nazi mystic philosopher Julius Evola, and former Chilean diplomat Miguel Serrano who likens the SS to initiates seeking the Holy Grail, provide the theoretical base of Nazi occultism. But it is ex-SS Wilhelm Landig's writings of the mythical Germanic homeland of Thule, an underground Arctic ice cap lab, where Nazi scientists build UFOs and prepare Nazi extraterrestrials to undo the Jewish threat.

Islamic Hate Groups: Bin Laden and the al Qaeda network, Egyptian Jihad, Hamas, Hizzbolah, PFLP, and several other groups are dedicated to fundamentalist Islam and politics of antisemitism, anti-Western values. Islamic hate groups believe the following. Israel and Jews are evil and must be destroyed. and the State of Palestine returned to Arabs. U.S., England, and Western nations must similarly be destroyed." The greatest enemies of the Islamic nation are the Jews, may Allah fight them … All spears should be directed at the Jews, at the enemies of Allah, the nation that was cursed in Allah's book. Allah has described them as apes and pigs, the calf-worshipers, idol-worshipers_"

Martyrdom for acts of destruction is believed to be rewarded in heaven." If he (the martyr) meets Allah, is forgiven with the first drop of blood; he is saved from the torments of the grave; he is saved from the Great Horror [of the day of judgment], and is crowned with the crown of glory, whose precious stone is better than all of this world and what is in it." Heaven consists of 80,000 servants and 72 wives (Buxom companions called "hurs" (in Arabic) who do not sleep, get pregnant, menstruate, spit, blow their noses or defecate). in pearl, aquamarine and ruby decorated dome with 'beakers full of sparkling wine, companions with big beautiful eyes,and gardens of tranquility.' The wine is nonintoxicating and one can consume 100 times more food and drink than on earth. Hell is occupied mostly by women who are sent there for ungratefulness to their husbands demands.

CONSEQUENCES OF ANTISEMITIC FOLKLORE

ANTISEMITIC LEGISLATION

Under Islam

If what I say is not true, may I become a Jew.
        —Muslim oath.

Dhimmis (Jews and Christians) were granted protection with the following restrictions.

Residence confined to designated areas
Limited worship. No proselytizing.
Specific trades.
Exempted from Military service
Paying poll (jizyah) and land taxes
Muslim men could marry Jewish women and own Jewish slaves.
Jews cannot marry Muslims
No desecrating Muslim scriptures or defaming the Prophet.
Restrictions on dress.
Prohibited from riding noble animals e.g. horses or camels,
Prohibited from carrying arms
Prohibited from holding public office,
Prohibited from building or repairing places of worship
Prohibited from mourning loudly
Prohibited from wearing shoes outside a Jewish ghetto.
Prohibited from building a dwelling higher than a Muslim's
Cannot testify against Muslim in a court of law.

Saudi Ministry of Tourism announces on its web site that visas to enter the country will not be issued to "Jewish people." (2004) Jews are not permitted citizenry in Jordan as of 1921 when Churchill signs Civil Law #6. The law states, "Any man will be a Jordanian subject if he is not Jewish." Since 1954, "any man in the West Bank will be a Jordanian subject if he is not Jewish." In Libya, Jews required to wear an identity badge and dismount from their donkey to greet a Muslim with "My Lord."

Under Christendom

To be a Jew is a crime.
        —Leon Poliakov

Special identification/badges/clothing (Fourth Lateran Council, 1215)
Cannot intermarry Christians
Cannot proselytize
Cannot eat together with Christians.
Food buying restrictions.
Jewish cooking illegal (Inquisition)
Christians forbidden to see Jewish doctors.
Cannot own property/Property confiscated,
Barred from crafts, guilds/professions.
Subject to special taxes
Cannot teach Hebrew (Russia)
Cannot enter military
Could not hold civic office or serve as elected officials
Could not be freemen in London
Could not attend university
Jewish physicians cannot treat Christians
Cannot act as agent for a contract
Cannot employ Christian servants
Cannot show themselves outside during Holy Week (Easter)
Ghettos/restricted areas of residence.
Cannot testify against Christians
Must attend church sermons
Forced conversions to Christianity or subject to death.

Burning of Jews at Nuremberg, from the Nuremberg Chronicle,
by Hartmann Schedel (1440–1514)

A MILLENNIUM OF ANTISEMITIC MYTH
(Under ISLAM)*

REGION	*MYTH*	*JEWISH DEATHS*
Fez; Marrarkesh Mor (1146, 1160)	Myth Unknown	120,000
Fez Mor (1033)	Sultan favors Jews and angers mob	6,000+
Granada Sp(1066)	Cleric objects to the Jew's power	5,000
Cordoba Sp (1010–1013)	Myth Unknown	1,000s
Morocco (1100s)	Converted and decimates communities	1,000s
Fez Mor (1276)	Ruler Indris II eradicates Jews	1,000s
Fez Mor (1465)	Jewish vizier offended Muslim woman	1,000s
Marrakesh Mor(1232)	Myth Unknown	1,000s
Marrakesh Mor (1864–1880)	Myth Unknown	300–500
Libya (1785)	Pasha Ali Burzi concern for Jewish secrets	100s
Algiers (1805); 1815;1830)	"Black Sabbath" Jewish prosperity	100s
Baghdad (1941)	Nazi instigated Farhud (pogrom)	187–400
Tripoli Libya (1945;1948;1967)	Myth Unknown	140/12/18
Egypt (1945; 1948)	Nationalism	10/70
Fez Mor (1912)	French Takeover	60–200
Damascus (1840)	Blood Libel	60 child
Fez Mor (1948)	Israeli Statehood	44 riots
Aden Yemen(1947)	Israel Partitioned	82 riots
Buenos Aires (1994)	Jewish Center AMIA bombing	85
Jaffe (1921)	Br. Mandate to Create Jewish State Announced	43 riots
Tetuan, Mor (1790)	Myth Unknown	40 killed

REGION	*MYTH*	*JEWISH DEATHS*
Taza, Mor (1903)	Myth Unknown	40 riots
Casablanca (1907)	Tribal rebellion	30
Constantine, Algeria (1934)	Nazi propaganda	25 riots
Demnat, Morocco (1875;1884)	Myth Unknown	20/riots
Debdou, Morocco (1875)	Myth Unknown	20
Tunis, (1869)	Jewish ghetto attack	18
Mashdad, Iran (1839)	Myth Unknown	15–18
Barfurush, Iran (1867)	Myth Unknown	15–18
Baghdad (1828)	Myth Unknown	10+ riots
Baghdad (1936)	Antisemitic Myth	10 riots
Kamishliye Syr (1967)	Myth Unknown	57
Constantine Alg (1934)	Myth Unknown	25 riots
Djerada, Oujda, Mor (1948)	Myth Unknown	43 riots
Damascus (1947;1949)	Israel Partitioned	12/30
Iran (1979–2000)	Accused as Zionist spies	13
Iraq (1969;1972)	Accused as Zionist spies	9/29

---

*Excludes injuries, rapes, lootings; forced conversions e.g Yemen (1165, 1678) Morocco (1275, 1465, 1790) Baghdad (1333, 1344), ghettoizations (19thC Algeria, Tunisia, Egypt, Libya, Morocco); property damage e.g. destruction of synagogues Egypt and Syria (1014, 1293, 1301) Iraq (845–859, 1344) Yemen (1676), book burnings and and rescue/ averted genocide e.g. 45,000 Yemen (1950) Excludes unknown death tolls: Allepo (1810,1947); Basra (1776); Beirut (1824); Antioch(1829); Harma(1829); Tripoli(1834); Jerusalem(1838); Rhodes(1840); Algiers (1805,1815, 1830); Les Nabeul, Tunisia (1880); Settat, Morocco (1903,1907). Excludes mass airlifts of 45,000 Yemen (1950). Excludes 4,000–5,000 in North African Nazi concentration camps. Excludes Buenos Aires Israeli Embassy (1992) attack killing 29).

A MILLENNIUM OF ANTISEMITIC MYTH
(IN CHRISTENDOM)*

REGION	MYTH	JEWISH DEATHS
Nazi, Europe (1939–1945)	Racial underminers	6,000,000
Chmielnicki, Rus (1648–1656)	Cossacks Rebel 'The Deluge'	100,000–300,000
Russian Rev/Civil War (1917–1922)	Nationalism	100,000–200,000
Odessa (1941)	Antonescu's Judeo-Communism	30,000
Rindfleisch/Armleder, Ger (1298/1336)	Host Desecration	20,000–100,000
Seville/Cordova Spain (1391)	Multiple religious/state myth	10,000–50,000
Poland/Bohemia(1290)	Unknown	10,000
Iasi, Romania (1941)	Pre-Nazi pogrom	13,000–15,000
Germany (1096) (1st Crusade)	Declared Heretics	12,000+
Granada (1066)	Joseph the Jew crucified	4,000–5,000
Seville (1391)	Archbishop Martinez	4,000
Prague (1389/1744)	Austrian military Easter Pogrom	3000, n/a
St. Petersburg (1905)	Bloody Sunday Pogrom	3000
Hungary (1919)	White Terror	3000
Strausbourg/Basel(1349)	Jews economic clout	2,000+ burned
Lisbon (1506)	A Jew questions a miracle after church service	2,000 mobs
France (1147)(2nd Crusade)	Heretics	100s-1000s
Germany (1189) (3rd Crusade)	Heretics	100s-1000s
England (1267)	Unknown	100s-1000s
Europe (1348–1350)	Black Death Accusation	1,000s+ burned
Inquisition(1288–1739)	Limpieza de Sangre (blood purity)	1,000s autodafe

REGION	MYTH	JEWISH DEATHS
Kiev (1113; 1736; 1768)	Grand Duke favoritism/post Cossack	1,00s-1000s
Toledo, Sp (1355)	Spanish Inquisition	1,200 riots
Proskurov, Vilna, Lvov(1919)	Myth Unknown	1,700+
Yalta/Lvov (1918)	Myth Unknown	900 drown/100s
Seville (1481–1488)	Crypto-Jews practicing Judaism	750
Nuremberg (1298)	Host Desecration	628
Nuremberg (1349)	Myth Unknown	562
Krakow-Kiecle-Rzeszow(1945, 1946)	Postwar Return/Blood Libel	500–1500**
Aquitaine Fr (1321)	Jews first charged as Christ's enemies	500+
Odessa (1905)	Patriotism questioned	400–800
York, Eng (1190)	Abbot Samson sermon Clifford Tower	57–600 burned
Palma, Majorca (1391)	Blood Libel	300 riots
Baden (1332)	Myth Unknown	300 burned
Vilnius (1826)	Myth Unknown	100s
Odessa (1821,1859, 1871, 1881)	Nationalism	100s
Bela Kun, Hun(1919)	Myth Unknown	100s murdered
Pforzheim (1285)	Myth Unknown	180 burned
Chinon, Fr (1321)	Blood Libel	160 buried alive
Bucharest (1801)	Blood Libel	128 riots
Brat-sur-Seine Fr (1191)	Blood Libel	100
Lima, Peru (1639)	Conversos (Forced Christian Converts)	80+ auto-da-fe
Soviet Union (1961–1963)	Economic Jewish Crimes Trials	68 executed
Kishinev/Homel Rus (1903–1905)	Blood Libel, Jew Money	29/49/339 killed

REGION	MYTH	JEWISH DEATHS
Russia (1881)	Czar executed	50 killed
Schaffhausen, Switz (1401)	Well Poisoning Ritual Murder	48 burned
Kiecle, Pol (1946)	Blood Libel	42 riots
Bloise Fr (1171)	Blood Libel	38 burned
Lisbon (1739)	Myth Unknown	35 executed
Fulda Ger(1235)	Blood Libel	34 riots
Casablanca (1907)	Tribal rebellion	30 massacre
Posing, Hun (1529)	Blood Libel	30 burned
Podolia, Rus (1919)	Myth Unknown Ukrainian army led	25 murdered
Mecklenburg, Ger (1492; 1350)	Host Desecration Well poisoning	24 burned, n/a
Lincoln, Eng (1255)	Blood Libel	18 executed
Odessa (1821; 1859; 1871;1881)	Myth Unknown	17+executed
Posen, Pol (1399)	Jews 'stealing and desecrating' Church property	13 elders & Rabbi
Spain (1482)	Trial for Jewish Black Magic	11 executed
Vistula Region (1407–1816)	Blood Libel	10+ execution.

---

*Excludes forced conversions, relocations, expulsions (15,000 Poland 1968), woundings, property damage, book burnings and rescue e.g Ethiopia (1984,1991). Excludes less than 10 killed e.g. Doctors Plot Soviet Union and Hungarian Pogrom (1946) "Jews make sausage of Christian children" 2 killed. The "Hep Hep" riots of Ger/Pol/Den (1819) triggered by emancipation fears. Killing and antisemitic violence in Neustettin (1881) Konitz blood libel (1900) and Berlin (1923). Excludes multiple Polish clergy blood libels (1598–1758) Excludes unknown death tolls e.g. Bialystock (1903); Catalonia (1358); Vienna (1405); Lublin (1598,1655); Brussels(1370); Cambrai(1402); Prague(1305); Marmor(1843); Smyrna(1864); Corfu(1894); SeredinoBuda (1918); Cochin (1662); Sicily (1391,1474); Changpu, China (1884); Thuringia (1303); Toulouse (1420); Sebastopol (1918); Tizsaeszlar (1882); Xanten (1882) Norwich UK (1190). **See Jan Gross (2006) *Fear,* New York: Random House

References

Ambrosewicz, J. & Oral-Bukowska, A. (1998) After the fall: Attitudes towards Jews in post-1989. Poland. *Nationalities Papers, 26,* 265–282.

Angenot, M. (1989) *Ce que l'on dit des Juifs en 1889: Antisemitisme et discourse social.* Montreal: Centre Interuniversitaire d'Etudes Europeennes

Abu-Rabia, A (2005) The evil eye and cultural beliefs among the Bedouin tribes of the Negev. Middle Eas*t. Folklore, 116*, 241–254.

Allen, S. L. (2002) *In the devil's garden.* New York: Ballantine

Ashliman D.L. (2004) *Folk and fairy tales.* Westport Greenwood Press

Bale, A (2003) Fiction of Judaism in England before 1290. In P. Skinner (Ed) *Jews in medieval Britain.* Rochester, NY: Boydell Press.

Bar-Itzhak, H (2001) *Jewish Poland-legends of origin.* Detroit: Wayne State University

Bartoszewski, W T (1984) *Ethnocentrism—beliefs and stereotypes: A sstudy of Polish-Jewish relations in the early 20th Century.* Unpublished doctoral dissertation. Cambridge University Press.

Bartrop, P R. (1987) "Good Jews" and "Bad Jews": Australian perceptions of Jewish migrants and refugees, 1919–1939. In W.D. Rubinstein's (Ed) *Jews in the sixth continent.* Sydney: Allen & Unwin, 169–184.

Basiura, E. (1997) *Jews of Poland in tale and legend.* Warsaw: Storyteller

Baum, SK (2008) The psychology of genocide. New York: Cambridge University Press

Baum SK & Nakazawa (2007) Antisemitism versus anit-Israeli sentiment, *Journal of Religion and Society, 9,* 1–8

Baum, S.K. (2007) Antisemitism as a mental disorder. In M. Fineberg, S. Samuels & M. W60eitzman (Eds)) *Antisemitism the generic hatred.* London: Vallentine Mitchell

Baum, S.K & Rudski, J. (2008) Antisemtism and superstition. *Journal of Contemporary Religion 23, 77–86.*

Bonfil, R (1988) The devil and the Jewish in Christian consciousness of the Middle Ages. In S. Almong (Ed) *Antisemitism through the ages.* Oxford: Pergamon

Boyes G (1996) Belief and disbelief: An examination of reactios to the presentation of rumour legends. In G Bennet and P. Smith (Eds) Contemporary legend: A reader. Pp 41–51 New York: Garland Publishing.

Burstein, S.A. (1959) Folklore, rumor and prejudice. *Folklore 70,* 361–381

Bynum C .W. (2004) The presence of objects. *Common Knowledge, 10,* 1–32

Cala, A (1995) *Studies on Polish Jewry.* Jerusalem: Magnes

Cohn, N.(1993) *Europe's inner demons.* Chicago: University of Chicago Press Rev.Ed.

Cohn, N.(1996) *Warrant for genocide.* London: Serif Rev. Ed.

Creasman, A.F. (2002) The Virgin Mary against the Jews: Anti Jewish polemic in the pilgrimage of the Schone Maria of Regensburg, 1519–25. *Sixteenth Century Journal, 33,* 963–980.

Czyzewka,M. (1994) The concept of the human nature nd the readiness for anti-Semitic behavior. Unpublished MA Thesis University of Wroclaw.

Dow, J.R. & Lixfeld, H. (1994) *The Nazification of an academic discipline.* Bloomington IL: Indiana University Press

Dundes, A. (1980) *Interpreting folklore.* Bloomington: Indiana University

Dundes, A. (1989) *Life is like a chicken coop ladder.* Detroit: Wayne State University Press

Dundes. A (1991) The ritual murder or blood libel legend: A Study of antisemitc victimization through projective invesrion. In Al Dundes (Ed) *The blood libel legend.* Pp 336–366. Madison: University of Wisconsin Press

Dundes, A (1997) *From game to war.* Lexington: Univeristy Press of Kentucky

Ellis, Bill (2001) *Aliens ghosts and cults.* Jackson: Univeristy Press of Mississippi

Fabre-Vassas, C. (1997) The singluar beast. New York: Columbia University Press

Fein, H. (1979) *Accounting for genocide.* New York: Free Press.

Fine. G.A. (1992) *Manufactuing tales.* Knoxville: Univeristy of Tennessee Press

Fine, G.A. (2001) *Difficult reputations.* Chicago: Univiersity of Chicago Press

Finkelkraut, A. (1994) *The imaginary Jew.* Lincoln: University of Kansas Press

Gilman, S.L. (1986) *Jewish self-hatred.* Baltimore: Johns Hopkins University

Ginzburg, C. (1991) *Ecstasies* Chicago:University of Chicago Press

Goldhagen, D.J. (1996) *Hitler's willing executioners.* New York: Knopf

Greenspoon, LJ & Le Beau, BF (Eds) (1996) *Representations of Jews through the ages.* Omaha: Creighton University

Gross, J.T. (2006) *Fear,* New York: Random House

Grosser Nagarajan, N (1999) *Jewish tales from Eastern Europe.* Lanham MD: Jason Aronson

Grosser Nagarajan, N (2005) *Pomegrante seeds.* Albuquerque: University of New Mexico Press

Hanak, P. (1985) A masokrol alkotott kep: Polgarosodas es etnikai eloitelek a Magyar tarsadalomban (a 19. szazad masodik feleben). *Szazadok 119,* 1079–1104.

Hanak P (1998) *The garden and the workshop*. Princeton: Princeton University Press

Hasan-Rokem, G & Dundes, A.(1986) *The wandering Jew*. Bloomington IN: Indian University Press

Herzog H. (1994) *The Jews as 'Others': On Communicative Aspects of Antisemitism*. Jerusalem:SICSA ACTA NO. 4,

Hultin NC (1988) The cruel Jew's wife: An Anglo-Irish ballad of the early Nineteenth Century. *Folklore, 99,* 189–203

Kamentsky, C. (1972) Folklore as a political tool in Nazi Germany. *Journal of American Folklore, 85,* 221–235

Kamenetsky, C. (1979) Folklore and ideology in the Third Reich. *Journal of the American Folklore, 90,* 168–178.

Kamenetsky, C. (1992) *The brothers Grimm and their critics.* Athens OH: Ohio University Press

Kofta, M. & Sedek, G. (2005) Conspiracy stereotypes of Jews during systemic transformation in Poland. *International Journal of Sociology, 35,* 40–64.

Kohno, T (1987) The Jewish question in Japan. *Jewish Journal of Sociology 29,* 37–54.

Kotek, J . (2004) Post-hHolocaust and antisemitism. JCPA #12 online. http://www.jcpa.org/phas/phas-21.htm)

Kovacs, A (1999) *Antisemitic prejudices in contemporary Hungary.* Jerusalem: SICSA ACTA #16

Krekovicova, E. (1997) Jewishness in the eyes of others: Reflection of the Jew in Slovak folklore. *Human Affairs,7,* 167–183

Kren, G.M. (1979) The Jews: The image as reality. *Journal of Psychohistory, 6,* 285–299

Lipson, S.L .(2001) *Re-imagining Grimms' fairy tales.* Unpublished doctoral dissertation. Pacifica Graduate Institute *DAI 63, 02A* 706.

Maccoby, H. (1996) *A pariah people*. London: Constable

Matard-Bonucci, M.A. (2005) *Antisemythes*. Paris: New World

Merback, M.B. (2005) Fount of mercy, city of blood: Cultic anti Judaism and the Pulkau Passion altarpiece. *The Art Bulletin, 87,* 589–642.

Mayo, L.A (1988) *The ambivalent image.* Rutherford NJ: Farleigh Dickenson University Press.

Merback, MB (2008) Beyond the yellow badge. Boston: Brill

Michlic, J, B. (2006) Poland's threatening other. Lincoln: Nebraska University Press

Mieder W (1982) Proverbs in Nazi Germany. *Journal of American Folklore 95,* 435–464

Mieder, W. (1997) *The politics of proverbs.* Madison: University of Wisconsin Press

Mieder, W. (1993) *Proverbs are never out of season.* New York: Oxford University Press

Montagu, A (1997) *Mans most dangerous myth,* Lanham MD: AltaMira

Morin, E. (1971) *A rumour in Orleans.* New York: Pantheon

Newall, V. (1973) The Jews as witch figure. In V. Newall (Ed) *The witch figure.* London: Routledge & Kean Paul.

Oisteanu, A (2001) *Image of the Jew in Romanian culture.* Bucharest: Humanitas

Oisteanu, A (in press) *The demonization of the Jew: A comparative study of ethnic imagology.*

Oke, M K(1986) Young Turks, freemasons, Jews and the question of Zionism in the Ottoman Empire (1908–1913). *Studies in Zionism,* 7, 199–218.

Opalski, M. (1986) The Jewish tavern keeper and his Tavern in 19th C Polish literature . Jerusalem: Zalman.

Ostow, M. (1996) *Myth and madness.* New Brunswick NJ Transaction

Parenti, M (2004) Jesus, Mel Gibson & the demon Jew. *The Humanist, 64,* 22

Peltzoltz L (1988) The eternal loser: The Jew as depicted in German folk literature. *Folklore, 99,* 28–47

Pendlebury. A. (2005) Portraying the Jew in First World War Britain. London: Vallentine Mitchell

Po-Chia, R (1992) *Stories of a ritual murder trial.* New Haven: Yale University Press

Perednik, G.D (2003) Naïve Spanish Judeophobia, *Jewish Political Studies Review,* 15, online.

Perry, M & Schweitzer, F. (2002) *Antisemitism.* New York: Palgrave Macmillan

Pinsker L (1882) Autoemancipation.www.mideastweb.org/autoemancipation.

Proud, J.K. (1997) Perrault, Petain and the politiciation of the fairy tale. *Europa,3,* 1–15

Ramaekers, J. (1990) De houding van Nederlandse katholieken tegenover de joden, 1900–1900–1940]. In Dik van Arkel's (Ed.) *Van oost naar west: Racisme als mondiaal verschijnsel.* Baarn:Ambo

Rappoport, A.S. (1937/1972) *Folklore of the Jews.* Detroit: Singing Tree Press

Resnick, I. M .(2000) Medieval roots of the myth of Jewish male menses. *Harvard Theological Review, 93,* 241–263

Rockaway, R. & Gutfeld, A (2001) Demonic images of the Jew in the Nineteenth Century United States. *American Jewish History, 89,* 355–381.

Rosenthal, D. (2001) The mythical Jew: Antisemitism, intellectuals and democracy in post-communist Romania. *Nationalities Papers, 29,* 419–439.

Ross, M. H. (1993) *The culture of conflict* New Haven Yale University Press

Rubin, M (1999) *Gentile tales.* New Haven: Yale University Press

Salamon, H. (1999) *The hyena people.* Berkeley: University of California Press

Shain, M. (1984) From Pariah to Parvenu: The anti-Jewish stereotype in South Africa, 1880–1910. *Jewish Journal of Sociology,* 26, 111–127.

Shindler, C. (2004) Reading the Guardian In T. Parfitt & Y Egorova (Eds) *Jews, Muslims and mass media.* London: RoutledgeCurzon

Singer, M & Santiago, S. (1991) Doing fieldwork in Mesoamerica: Mayan Indians images of Jews. *Jewish Folklore and Ethnology Review,* 13, 19–22.

Sivan, E. (1985) *Interpretations of Islam, past and present.* Princeton, NJ: Darwin Press

Smith, D. N (1996) The social construction of enemies: Jews and the representation of evil. *Sociological Theory,* 14, 203–240

Smith T.W. (2005) *Jewish distinctiveness in America.* New York: AJC

Starman, H. (2004) Jews and ideations about Jews in contemporary Slovenia: Research outline. *Razprave in Gradivo, 45,* 160–184.

Stav, A. (2000). *Peace: The Arabian caricature of antisemitic imagery.* Jerusalem: Gefen Books

Tractenberg, J.(1966/1983) *The devil and the Jews* New York: Philadelphia: Jewish Publication Society

Uriely, E. (2006) Jew-hatred in contemporary Norweign caricatures. JCPA online. http://www.jcpa.org/JCPA/Templates/ShowPage.asp?DRIT=3&DBID=1 &LNGID=1&TMID=111&FID=253&PID=0&IID=1256&TTL=Jew-Hatred_in_Contemporary_Norwegian_Caricatures

Weinberg, H (2007) So What is the social unconscious anyway?" *Group Analysis,* 40 307–322

Wistrich, R.S. (2005) "European antisemitism reinvents itself"PDF (2.62MiB), American Jewish Committee.

Wistrich, R.S. (1991) *Antisemtism: The longest hate.* New York: Schocken.

Zipes, J. (2002) *The Brothers Grimm.* New York: Palgrave Macmillan.

Zipes, J. (1991) *The operated Jew.* New York: Routledge

Endnotes

Passover and the Blood Libel http://www.nysun.com/article/30846 retrieved August 1, 2006

1. In actual fact, adults often told fables and folk tales to each other often in settings such as taverns, the fields and settings other than reading to children at night, Kamenetsky (1992) suggests that telling children folktales is less than 200 years old and probably began with the Grimm's first published work Kinder—und Hausmarchen in 1812. On the other hand Stit Thompson in The Folktale has noted "A large number of the tales in Grimm came from educated persons of the Grimm's own social circle who told the tales as they remembered them from childhood, when they had heard them from a nurse."

    Legends are defined as true stories based on history, while myths are partly true and involve gods and the supernatural. By contrast, folktales, fairy tales, sagas, and fables are fictional stories used to instruct. Though most folktales are fictional or based only very loosely on actual people or events, some, such as the popular tale about Johnny Appleseed, do originate in reality. Folk is equated with peasant, but can mean any group sharing one common factor (Dundes, 1980). For brevity's sake, the terms fables, fairy tales, myths and legends will be used interchangeably here, since when it comes to ethnic hate, all are treted as real. Unfortunately, this unchallenged readiness to accept myth as truth—even in the face of evidence to the contrary—creates optimum conditions in which hatred flourishes.

    While folklore can convey historical truth, for our purposes we are concerned with the falsehoods folklore can engender. As well there is a link betweeen orally circulating literary naratives and myth, legend and tales. I am more concerned with the end result of circulating antisemitic falsehoods and mythologies. By contrast, folklorists would concern themselves with the differences between a single authored fixed-form semi-literary printed tale circulated for propaganda purposes versus a tale that circulates from the people (Volk). While the people's social voice at times contradicted and countered Church and State influence, when it comes to circulating antisemitic falsehoods, most people believe the myths. For a more complete definition see Kamenetsky (1992, p.2)

2. See Bill Ellis' conclusions in Aliens, ghosts and cults p. xiv. Also see G.A. Fine's (20001) Manufacturing tales. Knoxville: Univerisity of Tennessee Press

3. http://ingeb.org/songs/oldmothg.html No specific writer has ever been identified as Mother Goose, and the first known mention of which appears in an aside in a versified chronicle of weekly happenings, that appeared regularly for several years, Jean Loret's La Muse Historique (in 1660): comme un conte de la Mere Oye ("Like a Mother Goose story"). One of the first contemporary incidences of censorship of Mother Goose may have been in 1969 when the Xerox Corporation and co-publisher Arno Press were pressured into withdrawing their Legendary Library Facsimile edition reprint of Mother Goose's Nursery Rhymes and Fairy Tales, originally published in 1895. This early version includes two rhymes, out of 217, that are offensive to African-Americans ("Ten Little Niggers," renamed "Ten Little Indians" in later editions and dropped altogether in new versions) and to Jews in the following. The concept of dirty Jew is interesting as well. The Jews were 'dirty' because restricted housing in Hamburg and Frankfurt were located near garbage dumps. The proverb captures the prohibition against the Jew's essence. "Whoever wants to keep his house clean, should shut his door to Jews and whores." The German obsession with feces and dirt, blood purity and nationalism soil segued nicely into the Nazi notion of Judenrein. Alan Dundes notes that during the 19th century, caricatures of Jewish baby defecating money into a pot surrounded by admiring Jews was popular. (Dundes, 1989 p. 125; 1991) Also see Fine (1992) .

4. amazon.com reviewer anonymous but echoes academic reviews see Ambrosewicz, & Oral-Bukowska (1998) who observed in Poland that people did not really know what a Jew was except that it was bad e.g. "If someone is my enemy then he is a Jew." (p.270)

Endnotes Chapter 1

1. 1 Volovici, L . (1994) Antisemitism in post-communist Eastern Europe: A marginal or central issue. Acta #5 Jerusalem: Hebrew University. p.5

2. Cohn-Sherbok, D (1992) The crucified Jew. Grand Rapids MI: William B Eerdman p.51

3. Oisteneau, in press

4. Wistrich, R; (1995) Is there a cure for antisemitism? Partisan Review p395

5. New Yorker 10/2/00 p.110)

6. New Yorker 10/02/00 p.110

7. US NEWS AND WORLD REPORT (2005) Mysteries of the mind 2/23 p.57

8. http://pewglobal.org/reports/display.php?ReportID=206 In 1938, an American poll found that 41% of Americans felt that Jews had too much power and by 1945, that number had increased to 58%. After Germans and Japanese, ordinary Americans rated Jews the next most disliked group blaming them for the Holocaust. (Kirkland, S; Greenberg, J & Pyszcynski, T. (1987) Further evidence of the deleterious effects of overheard derogatory ethnic labels: Derogation beyond the target. Personality and Social Psychology Bulletin, 13, 216–227. For social transmission see Georgina Boyes (1996)

Endnotes Chapter 2

1. Bushnaq, I (Ed) Arab folktales New York Pantheon, p.299

2. http://weekly.ahram.org.eg/2003/621/travel.htm Ell-Shamy H M (1980) Folktales of Egypt. Chicago: University of Chicago Press

3. H. El-Shamy's(1995) Folk Traditions of the Arab World, Indiana University.

4. http://memri.org/bin/articles.cgi?Page=archives&Area=sr&ID=SR01102

5. http://www.islamonline.com/cgi-bin/news_service/ fatwah_story.asp?service_id=444

6. http://www.mideasttruth.com/adtvtxt.html

7. http://www.jcpa.org/phas/phas-21.htm

8. www.calvin.edu/.../cas/gpa/images/lb/lb43–29.jpg

9. For a full account see Cohen, J.J. (2006) Hybridity, identity and monstronsity in medieval Britain: On difficult middles. New York: Palgrave Macmillan. Also Hasan-Rokem and Dundes's (1986) The wandering Jew.

10. The Bantu speaking Lemba tribe of southern Africa purports stronger DNA evidence than the Beta Israel. There is some compelling evidence for the Ibo of Nigeria as well. Other African Jews include the Bnai Ephraim of Nigeria, the Ba-Saa tribe of Cameroon. Some tribes such as the Abayudaya of Uganda have adopted and practiced Judaism since 1917. Other new Jews include the House of Israel Sefwi Wiawso and Sefwi Sui in Western Ghana and Rusape Zimbabwe.

11. Scheiber, A (1985) Essays on Jewish folklore and comparative literature. Budapest Akademiai Kiado) Also see Greenspan & LeBeau, (1996)

Endnotes Epilogue

1.   1 Isidore Loeb, 1889 cited in Dundes 1991, p.350. For a large collection, see the two volume set edited by Dan Ben-Amos. *Folktales of the Jews:* Tales from Eastern Europe (2007) and *Folktales of the Jews:* Tales from Separdic Dispersion (2006) Jewish Publication Society.

ADDITIONAL READING

Almong, S. (1988) *Antisemitism through the ages.* New York: Pergamon.

Baum, S.K. (in press) *The psychology of antisemitism.* New York: Cambridge University Press

Boonstra, J. Jansen, H. & Kniesmeyer, J. (1989)(Eds) *Antisemitism A history portrayed.* Amsterdam: Anne Frank Foundation

Bostom A (2008) (Ed) *The legacy of Islamic antisemitism.* Amherst: Prometheus

Bronner, S.J. (2007) *The meaning of folklore.* Logan: Utah State University Press

Campion-Vincent, V. (2005) *Organ theft legend.* Jackson MS: University Press of Mississippi

Chanes, J (2000) *A dark side of history.* New York: Anti-Defamation League

Cheyette B. & Valman, N. (2004) *The image of the Jew in European liberal culture 1789–1914.* Portland: Vallentine Mitchell

Goldstein, D. (2004) *Once upon a virus.* Logan: Utah State University Press

Felsenstein, F. (1995) *Antisemitc stereotypes.* Baltimore: Johns Hopkins University

Gidal, N. T. 1998) *Jews in Germany from Roman times to the Weimar republic.* Cologne: Konemann

Hoffman C., Bergamnn, W., & Smith, H.W. (2002) (Eds) *Exclusionary violence.* AnnArbor: University of Michigan

Perry M & Schweitzer, F (2007) *Antisemtic myths.* Bloomington: Indiana Universiy Press

Rosnow, R.L. & Hantula, D.A. (2006) *Advances in social and organizational psychology.* Mahwah NJ: Lawrence Erlbaum

Wycoff, D. (1996) Now everything makes sense. Complicating the contemporary legend picture. In G. Bennett & P. Smith (Eds) *Contemporary legend: A Reader.* New York: Garland Publications

978-0-595-48140-8
0-595-48140-X